Practical Deer-stalking

By the same author

Deer and their Management in the Deer Parks of Great Britain and
Ireland
The Deer Stalking Grounds of Great Britain and Ireland
The Deer of Great Britain and Ireland
Deer Stalking in Scotland
Deer of the World
The Wild Goats of Great Britain and Ireland
The Ancient White Cattle of Britain and their Descendants
Hunting and Stalking Deer in Britain through the Ages
Hunting and Stalking Deer throughout the World
The Whitehead Encyclopedia of Deer

G Kenneth Whitehead

Practical Deer-stalking

**Line drawings by
Roger McPhail**

Constable · London

First published in Great Britain 1986
by Constable and Company Ltd
3 The Lanchesters, 162 Fulham Palace Road
London W6 9ER
Copyright © 1986 by G Kenneth Whitehead
ISBN 0 09 474030 5
Paperback edition 1986
Reprinted 1998
Printed in Great Britain by
St Edmundsbury Press Ltd
Bury St Edmunds, Suffolk

A CIP catalogue record for this book
is available from the British Library

Contents

Illustrations

Note all photographs by the author except number 14, which is by
   Raymond E. Chaplin.

Sketches and Diagrams

Acknowledgements

My first introduction to stalking was in 1930 on the Mull of Kintyre when my uncle very kindly arranged for me to go out with the keeper to shoot a Sika stag. Two years later, as the keeper was required on the grouse moor, I was sent out on my own, and after a long search, eventually stalked up to a party of stags and achieved my first right and left.

This, briefly, is the manner in which I became initiated as a deerstalker, but I find it impossible adequately to express my gratitude not only to my uncle, for having first introduced me to this wonderful sport, but also to the many friends who subsequently during the past fifty years or so have been kind enough to invite me to stalk on their estates and share their knowledge. But for them this little book would probably never have been written, and I only hope I have done justice to my mentors.

Introduction

A good shot is not necessarily a good stalker – but he will probably be able to make the most of his opportunities. To increase those opportunities, however, he must also have experience, and whilst satisfaction, but little knowledge, will be gained from a successful stalk, it is from mistakes that real knowledge stems and every failure should improve one's knowledge, so that when faced with a similar situation the mistake will not be repeated.

With half a century of stalking behind me, and well over a thousand carcases into the larder, many of which I have had to butcher myself, I have certainly made my full quota of mistakes, and it is in the belief and hope that some of the lessons learned will now be of some help to those fortunate individuals who are just about to enter the world of the deerstalker that I have written this small book.

Even though it is over fifty years since I shot my first stag, I still get a thrill when a difficult stalk is nearing completion. In those early days, apart from a fortnight's holiday in the highlands, time for stalking was mainly limited to odd weekends, and no hour of daylight, or yard of ground on which I had permission to stalk was wasted. If a deer was shot in a difficult place for extraction what of it! I was young, reasonably strong and tireless in those days, and if it could not be dragged out it could always be cut up and carried out piecemeal. Today, I must admit, I manage to find a number of excuses for not trying to shoot a large deer in a really difficult spot for retrieval.

Stalking, particularly roe stalking, with its dawn and dusk outings into the forest, is an unsociable sport better suited to the loner than to one happiest when surrounded by fellow sportsmen, or loath to leave a warm bed. Still hunting in woodland requires one hundred per cent concentration, and this can only be achieved when on one's own.

Much of stalking is really common sense and can be self-taught, for no matter how many books may be read on the subject – and I hope this one will, nevertheless, be included – real sound knowledge is only to be gained from experience in the field.

Apart from rifle, ammunition and binoculars, one of the most important pieces of equipment of the woodland stalker is the alarm clock, for much of his activity will be centred around dawn. Yet despite the importance of the 'early call', so far as I am aware not a single book on stalking is able to provide information on this matter. True, many of the daily papers do give sunrise and sunset times, but these refer only to Greenwich Mean Time which is not going to be very helpful to anyone intending to stalk in the west of England or north of Scotland now or at some future date. For the first time, therefore, in Appendix A information is available for sunrise and sunset times for twelve different areas in England and Scotland throughout the twelve months of the year, and I would like to record my thanks to B. S. Hope of the Nautical College, Fleetwood, for having prepared this information for me.

A lot of the information contained in this book will, no doubt, seem obvious to the reader, as it does to me today. Forty or fifty years ago, however, it was not so, and there is no doubt that with 'hind sight' – and 'buck' sight also, for that matter – many more stalks would have succeeded.

You may not be able to ensure one hundred per cent success with every stalk attempted, but you can, at least, ensure that when the moment of truth arrives and the shot is taken, the rifle will shoot straight – so keep it zeroed by frequent testing at the target. One must, however, always be mindful of the fact that the last chance of a shot before the light fails is also the best chance to wound, so if there is any doubt don't take it. The fact that it may be your last chance that day does not in any way mitigate the circumstances, for no shot should be taken unless the outcome is as certain as any shot can be.

Before anyone can shoot a deer he will have to acquaint himself with the law relevant to the country in which he intends to stalk. Unfortunately, legislation regarding the shooting of deer in Great Britain is unnecessarily complicated, for not only are close-seasons in Scotland different from those in England and Wales, but so also are the legality of certain weapons and ammunition. In fact, one could have the somewhat farcical situation in late October where a roe stalker in southern Scotland, armed with his .222 rifle, could quite legally take aim at a doe standing on the border which, in being shot, collapsed and died on the English side, by which time it would have been killed out of season by an illegal weapon in England! In Appendix B will be found a summary of the laws which control the shooting of deer throughout Great Britain and Ireland.

The British Association for Shooting and Conservation (BASC) in collaboration with the British Deer Society (BDS) have issued a *Deer Stalker's Code* which should be studied by every young stalker. Copies are available, free of charge, from both organisations.

Training is vital, and any stalker would undoubtedly benefit by attending one of the short two to five day courses on woodland stalking that are run by the Game Conservancy or BASC (in conjunction with the Forestry Commission). A five day residential course on hill stalking is run each autumn on the island of Rhum by the British Field Sports Society (BFSS) in conjunction with the Red Deer Commission (RDC) but this is primarily intended for the professional stalker trainee. Anyone interested in attending any of these courses should contact the appropriate organisation.

In addition to the above, the St Hubert Club of Great Britain, which was probably the first organisation in the UK to appreciate the value of stalker training, has also been running courses for its members for over twenty years.

From the day you shoot your first deer, start keeping a Deer Stalking Register or Diary in which should be recorded not only brief details as to date, locality, species and sex, but also time of day, weather, wind, weight and any other brief details of interest to the stalker. Photographs of any unusual head also add interest.

Any deer shot should be given a reference number which will be entered on a large scale map. Over the years it is surprising what useful information can be obtained from this Diary, for seasonally deer are repetitive in their habits, and you will soon discover which areas of your ground are likely to be most productive in any particular month or weather conditions.

And finally, having shot a good trophy, it is as well to know how to prepare it for mounting, and suggestions are made in chapter 7 as to how to achieve this.

Quite apart from a lasting memento of a good stalk, a well mounted head can be an attractive wall decoration – a badly cut and discoloured skull is an eyesore!

Good hunting!

1

Firearms and Ammunition

Choice of rifle – Sighting-in a rifle – Care of the rifle –
Ammunition – Rifle slings – Rifle covers

Note: In this section, to fall in line with many ballistic tables, distances, etc. are given in imperial with metric equivalent.

(a) *Choice of rifle*

There are many good rifles for deer stalking and it would be wrong to say that any particular rifle is *the* best. Indeed, it would be fair to say that once the rifle has been zeroed, it is only as good as the person using it.

There is no doubt that a really good shot, who can guarantee to place his shot every time in a vital spot on the deer, can get away with a much lighter calibre than the indifferent performer who has to rely on the weight of the bullet to stop the deer should a vital spot have been missed. The experts are, unfortunately, in the minority and for the *average* deerstalker, therefore, I would recommend a rifle of calibre of not less than .275 (7 mm.) for all species of deer in Britain. The .30-06 is also an excellent weapon particularly as there is a range of bullet weights available.

In selecting a suitable rifle for deer stalking one must be guided not only by one's bank balance but also by the species of deer for which it will be used.

Another point which one must consider in buying a rifle is the availability of ammunition, for there is no point in buying a second-hand rifle, no matter how good its condition may be, if the ammunition is a discontinued line.

In selecting a suitable bullet for the rifle it should be remembered that those of light construction tend to break up or get deflected more easily by contact with twigs etc. than the heavier bullet, and if a bone is hit, tissue damage may be more severe.

On the other hand, the heavier bullet may well do less damage to the carcase on a light framed deer.

Weight of rifle will also have to be considered, and bearing in mind that the heavier rifle is easier to hold steady in a high wind and doesn't 'kick' as much, I would suggest that the rifle should weigh not more than about 3.4 kg. (7½ lb.), for the addition of a telescope sight will add a further 0.34 to 0.57 kg. (¾ to 1¼ lb.) dependent on the type of 'scope fitted.

Whatever rifle you finally decide to use, a careful study should be made of the ballistic and range tables that are issued by the various manufacturers of ammunition, and this is most important should you select a rifle for which there is a wide range of ammunition to choose from. For instance, there is a choice of four or five different bullet weights, ranging from 110 gr. to 220 gr. for the .30-06 and ballistics of each may be affected by the type of point, such as Pointed, Soft-point, Silver-tip etc. on the bullet. It is not sufficient, therefore, to go into a gun shop and simply ask for, say, a box of .30-06 ammunition without stating *exactly* not only the weight and type of bullet required, but also the make, for ballistics vary slightly from one manufacturer to another.

Having decided, therefore, on the type of ammunition that suits your requirements best, *stick* to it, and whenever a fresh supply is received, check the batch number, and should it be different to the previous batch, then it is a wise precaution to test it on the range, for mass produced factory supplies can vary slightly from time to time. This is particularly important when the fresh batch comes from a different manufacturer.

(b) *Sighting-in a rifle*

It is essential that any sighting-in should be carried out with the *actual* cartridge and bullet to be used on the hill. It is useless to sight-in a cartridge that has a different bullet weight or different muzzle velocity.

People who are unfamiliar with ballistics do not realise the extent to which a bullet will fall once it has passed the 100 yards (90 metres) mark, which is the ideal range at which to shoot a deer. A hundred yards is the range at which a rifle is generally zeroed, and also the range at which a newcomer to the hill will probably be tested out before being allowed to shoot a stag.

Before the war, in the pre-telescope-sight days, anyone getting a good group with open or iron sights on the 100 yard range target, would probably perform equally well on the hill, for there was not the same temptation to shoot at longer ranges when the distinctive features of a deer would be barely discernible at, say, 200 yards (182 metres) or more. Now, however, with the telescope sight, and in particular one of the varipower models, the crosswires look as clear behind the shoulder of a stag at 250 yards (228 metres) as at half this range, and the 'rifle' is, therefore, tempted to shoot, not realising that by the time the bullet reaches the target it may well have dropped by at least 10–12 in. (25–30 cm.) below the point of aim. The result, hopefully, will be a miss, but more than likely a stag with broken foreleg will be seen to limp away.

For woodland stalking, sighting-in at 100 yards is the ideal range, for few shots will be taken beyond this, and indeed, the majority will be nearer 70 yards (64 metres) when the difference between point of aim and strike is less than ½ in. (1.2 cm.) – an acceptable error for our two smaller deer, the Muntjac and Water-deer. Furthermore, any error under 100 yards will be high rather than low, so should a shot be high, unless a complete miss has occurred, the back bone will probably be shattered and this, even though not immediately fatal, will completely immobilise the deer.

For open hill stalking the best range to zero a rifle is about 200 yards, for even when a shot has to be taken at half this range, the line of flight of a bullet weighing 150 gr. or less will not be more than about 2½ in. (6.3 cm.) high, and this would certainly account for the deer.

Figure 1 illustrates the trajectory paths taken by 150 gr. and 220 gr. .30-06 calibre bullets, when fired at stags at ranges of 100, 200 and 300 yards, the rifle having been zeroed at 100

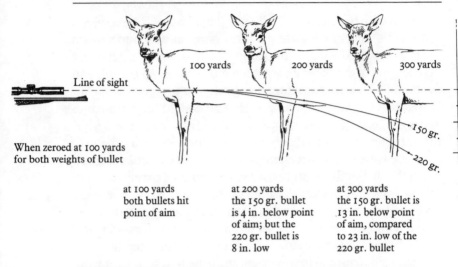

Line of sight

100 yards   200 yards   300 yards

When zeroed at 100 yards
for both weights of bullet

150 gr.

220 gr.

at 100 yards	at 200 yards	at 300 yards
both bullets hit point of aim	the 150 gr. bullet is 4 in. below point of aim; but the 220 gr. bullet is 8 in. low	the 150 gr. bullet is 13 in. below point of aim, compared to 23 in. low of the 220 gr. bullet

Figure 1 Trajectory of 150 gr. bullet as compared to that of 220 gr. bullet when fired from .30-06 rifle, both weights having been zeroed at 100 yards.

yards, at which range both bullet weights will hit the same spot. At 200 yards, although the lighter bullet has dropped by about 4.3 in. (10.9 cm.) it should still have accounted for the deer, but the point of impact for the 220 gr. bullet would have been some 3½ in. (8.9 cm.) lower and the beast would certainly have required a second shot. At 300 yards, however, both bullets would have missed the target completely, the 150 gr. bullet being some 13 in. (33 cm.) below the point of aim, and the heavier bullet 24 in. (61 cm.). At this latter range, to compensate for the drop, had the aim with the lighter bullet been taken along the line of the deer's back, bullet impact would have been some 13 in. (33 cm.) below the shoulder line, and therefore correctly placed. With the heavier bullet, however, for a heart shot at this range, the point of aim would have had to be in space some 12 in. (31 cm.) above the shoulder, which would be more or less guess work. At 400 yards (366 metres) the 150 gr. bullet will have dropped some 17½ in. (44.5 cm.) and the 220 gr. bullet 41 in. (104 cm.), the drop thereafter being progressively greater as the distance increases. If more people, therefore, realised this, fewer deer would be missed or wounded, and fewer people would be able to boast of having shot a deer at 500 yards (457 metres)! They may well have done so, but it was not good shooting, but a fluke. Shots at such ranges should only be taken in an effort to prevent a wounded beast getting away, and to do so the shooter must be familiar with the ballistics of his ammunition, and aim accordingly.

There is no doubt that trigger pressure plays an important part in shooting and it is mainly responsible for indifferent shooting by an established good shot when using a strange weapon. Generally speaking it can be said that the lighter the pressure, the easier it is to shoot accurately, the ultimate being the 'set trigger' – often referred to as the 'hair trigger'. Whilst a 'set trigger' is the best for shooting from a 'High-seat', it cannot be considered safe for stalking deer under Scottish conditions, which involve a considerable amount of crawling, and unless the owner of the rifle is *completely* familiar with the workings of a 'set trigger', and how to make it safe once set, accidental discharge could easily occur. I am of the opinion, therefore, that a conventional firing mechanism with a trigger pressure of 3½ lb. (1.6 kg.) is probably ideal for all deer shooting in Britain.

Many new rifles, when supplied, may have a trigger pressure set at 6 or 7 lb. (2.7 to 3 kg.) so when taking over a new weapon one of the first tests before sighting-in should be to have the trigger pressure tested and adjusted to your choice of pressure.

You can check the pressure by holding the rifle, muzzle down, in a vertical position and pulling the trigger with a lightweight Salter fisherman's spring balance, noting the maximum weight required to fire the rifle. Any adjustment required to bring the pressure to your requirements, however, will have to be done by a gunsmith.

Most stalking rifles are fitted with a sporting trigger which is somewhat straighter in design than the match rifle trigger. The amount of digital pressure required to squeeze the trigger will

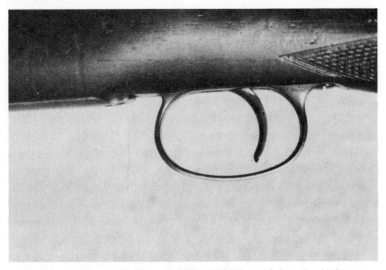

1(a) Most stalking rifles have a trigger that is straighter in design than one fitted to a match rifle for target work.

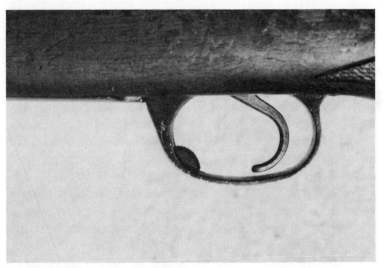

(b) The deeper curving trigger of the latter ensures that digital pressure is always applied at the same point.

vary in accordance with the part of the trigger to which the pressure is being applied. For instance, far less pressure is required if pressure to the trigger is applied at its tip rather than near the base. The shape of the deeper curving match trigger helps to ensure that digital pressure, whether in summer or begloved in winter, is always applied at the same point, which is not always the case with the straighter trigger. I have, therefore, had match triggers fitted to all my rifles, and having also standardised on 3½ lb. (1.6 kg.) pressure, results have been very rewarding.

Should your rifle retain its open sights it is essential that there should be some protection for the foresight, particularly when the rifle is being carried in a canvas cover. The best type of foresight guard is one that is permanently attached to the rifle, and can be hinged out of the way when firing the rifle. Spring clip-on guards are inclined to spring off and get lost.

Some foresight protectors consist of a leather cap which can be slipped over the muzzle-end of the rifle, being held in position by a leather thong, and which is also useful to prevent rainwater passing down the barrel. It can, however, be very easily overlooked when using a telescope sight, as vision through the 'scope will be above the protector cap. To prevent this happening, a piece of coloured tape tied in a bow can be attached to the protector, and will remain visible through the 'scope as a reminder to remove the protector.

To prevent rainwater, snow or foreign bodies etc. entering the bore of the barrel during a crawl, a useful tip is to cover the bore with a piece of insulating tape, and this offers no resistance to the bullet when the rifle is fired. Generally speaking, however, until near the firing point it is best to keep the cover on the rifle, as it will help to keep the 'scope dry as well.

Should, however, you unfortunately get some peat or earth lodged down the end of the bore when no rod is available, this can often be removed by sucking it out from the barrel end, rather than by attempting to blow it out from the breach – an almost impossible task without a tube to insert into the bore. Remember, however, to *UNLOAD* the rifle – something which can, in the panic of the occasion, be very easily overlooked when the blockage occurs during the last few yards of a crawl just prior to the shot.

It is surprising the number of people who never trouble to take any target practice, but I am sure if they did, better shooting would result. Some may only have the chance to fire at three or four stags per season – some even fewer – and this small number of shots per year is unlikely to keep anyone in the best of form.

Target practice is not only to familiarise the shooter with his weapon, recoil and trigger pressure etc. but also to assure him that the rifle and 'scope are properly zeroed, and should any miss occur the fault will lie with the shooter and not the rifle. Accidents do happen, and even though the rifle may have been shooting spot-on at the end of the previous season the 'scope may have received a jolt in the meantime, and it is best to test and be sure than not, and be sorry. One should, therefore, zero the rifle after any accidental knock, or unaccountable miss, and preferably this should be done before a further stalk is attempted. As a temporary measure the bolt can be removed and the rifle 'boresighted' (see page 47). For the stalker of highland Red deer, each stalk follows a more or less set pattern, with the majority of shots being taken in a prone position, which is familiar to anyone who has shot with a rifle, so frequent practice is probably not so important.

For the Roe stalker in woodland terrain, however, the prone shot is the exception, and whilst the majority of shots in May and June can be taken in a sitting position, those in late summer or autumn, owing to the height of the undergrowth and bracken, if not taken from a 'High-seat' will often have to be taken from a standing position, with or without the assistance of a tree or stick for support. Many rifle shots have never had to take a standing shot and the first occasion should not be at a deer but at a target, so as to be better prepared to cope with the situation when it occurs in the forest.

Although good grouping on the target will not necessarily ensure similar results on deer, it will at least confirm that if a miss should occur on the hill, it is due to no fault of the rifle but to the man behind it.

When zeroing a rifle, it is essential to use a rest, and one should not be satisfied until a group of not less than three shots can be placed on a 10 cm. (4 in.) square at 100 metres (109 yards). A permanent target in the form of a life-size 'iron stag' or 'iron buck' is useful for a guest to test out a strange rifle. Whilst the stag itself can be constructed of not less than 1.5 cm. (⅝ in.) mild steel, the target area around the shoulder should be reinforced with armour plating, for the former will not stand up to the modern bullet. To avoid ricochets, the target should be leaning *forward* so as to direct spent bullets into the ground. For measurements see figure 2. For a Roe buck, reduce measurements by approximately 40 per cent.

(c) *Care of the rifle*

In the old days it was essential to boil out the barrel as soon as possible after firing the rifle, but today this is unnecessary as modern cartridges are fitted with non-mercuric caps and, being non-rusting, these really make regular boiling out unnecessary. However, if many shots have been fired no harm could be done if the barrel was boiled out at the end of the season before being stored away. If the rifle is in danger of being stored in a damp room, a thin coating of petroleum jelly is to be recommended. During the season the rifle should be cleaned every day it is taken out, irrespective of whether a shot has been fired or not. Any oil left in the barrel overnight should be removed before going out. If the rifle is in constant use, from time to time the barrel should be well scrubbed out with a bristle brush dipped in one of the cleaning fluids and then wiped out clean and dried with a rag or tow before being lightly oiled. This will be quite sufficient to keep it free from rust.

If there is any rust or fouling in the barrel, this should be removed with a wire brush dipped in a cleaning fluid.

The extractor mechanism, magazine and other accessible

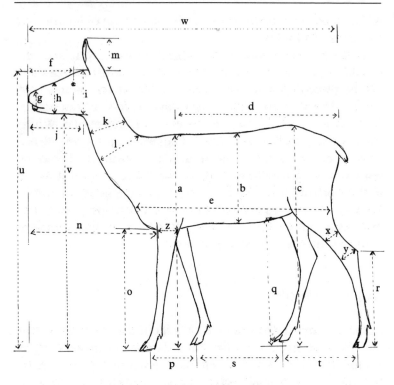

Outline Measurements for 'Iron' Stag

	cm.	in.		cm.	in.		cm.	in.
a.	111.8	44	j.	29.2	11½	s.	47.0	18½
b.	47.6	18¾	k.	20.0	7⅞	t.	43.2	17
c.	109.2	43	l.	26.0	10¼	u.	146.0	57½
d.	88.9	35	m.	14.3	5⅝	v.	122.6	48¼
e.	106.6	42	n.	90.2	35½	w.	177.2	69¾
f.	25.4	10	o.	60.9	24	x.	9.5	3¾
g.	8.6	3⅜	p.	28.0	11	y.	11.1	4⅜
h.	14.3	5⅝	q.	67.0	26⅜	z.	11.4	4½
i.	23.8	9⅜	r.	49.0	19¼			

If desired, a cast antler can be attached to the head to complete the 'stag' silhouette.

Figure 2 Sketch and measurements of 'Iron stag' target.

moving parts should also be lightly oiled with a fine quality gun oil, and the outside of the barrel should be wiped down with an oily rag. An old tooth-brush is useful for cleaning the extractor mechanism, etc. All oil and cleaning fluid, however, must be wiped out of the barrel before shooting.

When putting the rifle away into store at the end of the season, it is a wise precaution to wear an old pair of kid gloves, or hold only the stock after having given the outside of the barrel a final wipe down with an oily rag – otherwise perspiration from the hands may get on to the barrel and cause rust.

The stock can be given a light rub over with a slightly oily rag, but excess application of oil to any woodwork should be avoided.

It should be unnecessary to say that on the hill or in the forest, the rifle should always be carefully handled and never left in a place where it can be knocked over by a car door or exuberant hound.

(d) *Ammunition*

Ammunition for deerstalking must be of soft-nosed or hollow-nosed type, solid service ammunition being quite unsuitable and illegal.

Unfortunately the calibre and type of ammunition that it is legal to use on deer is not uniform throughout England, Wales and Scotland and reference should be made to Appendix B (page 168) which briefly summarises the provisions of the Acts relating to firearms and ammunition.

Within the requirements of these Acts the stalker has a wide range of cartridges from which to select, and as stated on page 22, having made your choice, stick to it. It must be remembered, also, that no rifle ammunition can be bought without producing the Firearm Certificate on which the particulars will have to be entered, so if you are going away on a stalking trip and may require to purchase ammunition, be sure to take your certificate with you. The best safeguard is to take sufficient ammunition with you, remembering that you *may*, as the result of an accident, have to re-zero your rifle, so at least an extra ten rounds should be taken for this purpose.

As to the number of rounds one takes to the hill, this is rather a matter of personal opinion, dependent really on the number of deer you *might* be required to kill. On some of the larger forests the stalking party may sometimes take to the hill with perhaps a Snowtrac or three or four ponies and with reasonable luck, there should be three or four carcases back in the larder that evening. With the prospect of four stags, I suggest fifteen to twenty rounds should be taken, but if only one or two stags are to be killed, ten rounds should be sufficient. This does not mean that one expects to use five rounds for every stag killed – one, normally, should be sufficient but accidents sometimes happen and it is always comforting to have a few rounds to spare, especially when – heaven forbid – a stag with a broken foreleg has to be dealt with, which may entail one or two running shots.

As to the number of rounds placed in the magazine, unless one is planning to take more than one beast from a herd, if the capacity of the magazine is five, then I would normally charge it with four, in the belief that it is best not to keep the magazine spring under full tension for long periods. Whatever number, however, you prefer to put in the magazine, make it a practice to *always* keep to that number, for should you on one occasion put in one more than usual, when the time comes to unload the rifle, when the 'usual' number has been ejected, unless the rifle has been 'proved' – that is working the bolt backwards and forwards three or four times – there is a good chance of a round being left in the magazine. After working the bolt, before it is finally closed, depress the trigger, thus releasing the spring. This is far safer than pulling the trigger after the bolt has been closed.

The modern cartridge carton is quite useless to take on the hill for it soon gets squashed or turned into pulp by continual wetting. Cartridges, therefore, should always be carried in a proper leather pouch, or in some sort of box or small bag, and not just left loose to jangle about in the pocket. An empty cartridge carton, however, should be retained in the gun room so that when the pouch or whatever was used in the forest is emptied there is a correctly identified carton available in which to keep the loose rounds.

If you own two rifles of different calibre, but use the same cartridge pouch for both, you will probably find that the cartridge for the smaller calibre will tend to fall out of the holding compartment. Beware of putting a tube of thick paper or card as packing in each compartment to reduce the circumference for there is a very real chance, as I myself once experienced, that the tube will be withdrawn along with the cartridge and placed in the magazine of the rifle, and should it work its way into the bore a very serious accident could result when the rifle was fired.

Modern ammunition is remarkably free from misfires, and when one does occur it is often the fault of the shooter rather than the cartridge. On three occasions, in my anxiety to make as little noise as possible, I have had misfires caused by my failure to close the bolt properly, the first occurring in Africa where I found myself standing face to face with a buffalo. On the second occasion a small piece of twig became lodged between the bolt handle and woodwork.

The third and most recent occasion was caused by the strap for the telescope sight cover preventing the safety catch from being fully released. As on the other occasions, the cap was dented by the striker, but insufficiently for ignition.

As to the number of shots that one should fire at a deer, I am of the opinion that if, after missing with a first shot, the second should also be wide of the target, no further shots should be attempted, even if it might prove to be third time lucky. The sound of one shot causes relatively little disturbance, but on hearing two shots, any deer in the locality will start to take real notice, and if their anxiety is confirmed by a third shot, they soon take the hint and take flight, probably finishing up on your neighbour's ground. With a wounded stag, however, the situation is quite different and no trouble or ammunition should be spared until the unfortunate beast has been accounted for. It is always better therefore, to take rather too many than too few cartridges with you to the hill.

After completion of one stalk, and before starting a second, make sure that the magazine is fully reloaded, for you *may* be faced with a wounded beast and an empty magazine.

And finally, should you at any time be reduced to your last cartridge, *never* fire at a fresh stag, for you will be helpless should a wounded deer result. Even when reduced to two cartridges, it should be the rule never to fire at a beast more than 100 metres (109 yards) away so as to ensure that should a second shot (which will be your last) be required, the range will still be short enough to *ensure* a kill.

It is, perhaps, unnecessary to say that one can never handle firearms too safely, and although every rifle is fitted with a safety catch, when this is 'off' should the rifle receive a severe jolt, this may release the firing mechanism irrespective of whether the trigger had been touched. Always, therefore, ensure that the 'Safety catch' is 'on safe' and never carry a loaded rifle in a vehicle or on a pony.

If during a crawl you happen to be following your stalker but carrying the rifle yourself, be certain to see that the safety catch is on and that the barrel is not pointing up your stalker's backside. For this reason, and for their own peace of mind, stalkers generally prefer to carry the rifle themselves until the firing point is reached. It may seem a lazy way of stalking for the sportsman, but it does prevent the chance of what could be a very serious accident.

(e) *Rifle slings*

Both the rifle and the rifle cover should have separate slings attached, for it is much easier to carry the rifle, whether within its cover or without, when slung from the shoulder, than carried by hand at the trail. Rifle slings, generally about 2.5 to 3.7 cm. (about 1 to 1½ in.) in width, can be either canvas or leather, but the latter is undoubtedly the best, particularly if made of plaited leather, which will help to prevent it slipping from the shoulder. Slings must be fitted with an adjustable buckle, and can be attached to the eyelet on the fore end of the rifle either by a brass stud or leather thong. An advantage of the thong attachment over the more conventional metal eyelet and swivel is that it is completely silent – an essential factor when 'still hunting' in woodland. Unfortunately, the leather thong has a very limited life and unless constantly inspected, may break on the hill, causing serious damage to the rifle and 'scope should it fall on rocky terrain. The brass stud attachment is certainly more reliable, but here again, accidents can happen if the stud is not first inserted into the slit nearest the end of the sling with the larger end next to the rifle (and not into the second hole) as this will ensure that should the smaller end of the stud work out of the slot in the sling, the stud will be retained in the end of the sling, thus preventing it slipping out of the eyelet and causing the rifle to fall (see fig. 3(a) and (b)).

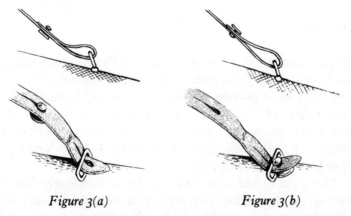

Figure 3(a)   *Figure 3(b)*

In securing a sling to the rifle, make sure that the brass stud is first inserted into the slit nearest the end of the sling, and not into the second slit, for should the smaller end of the stud, when carrying the rifle, slip out of its slit, the strap will slip out of the eyelet (a), causing the rifle to fall to the ground. If, on the other hand, the smaller end of the stud slips out of the second slit on the sling, the stud itself will be retained in the slit and thus prevent the sling slipping through the eyelet (b).

Frequently check the straps, particularly at the point of attachment to the rifle, to see that there is no undue wear. If there is any sign of wear, the sling should either be replaced, or if the worn bits are near the end, the sling can be shortened by cutting off the worn part and fresh perforations made for the brass stud.

Periodically after cleaning, leather straps and slings should be wiped over with saddle soap, and a wax leather dressing applied to retain flexibility. Should, however, the sling or strap become brittle with age or neglect, it is possible to restore some flexibility by first applying lanolin or castor oil mixed with about 30 per cent methylated spirit. After allowing about 24 hours for penetration, follow up with further applications of warm castor oil or lanolin (about 110°F or 43°C) until flexibility has been restored, when the wax and leather dressing should then be applied.

(f) *Rifle covers*

In Scotland it is the custom to carry one's rifle in a cover until such time as the firing point is about to be reached.

It is most important that the cover is *very* loose fitting, for withdrawal of a rifle from a tight-fitting cover, particularly when wet, can be very irksome and time-wasting. If the rifle is fitted with a telescope sight, the cover should be wide enough to take both the rifle and sight.

I have yet to find a canvas cover that is completely rainproof and unless drying facilities are extremely good, a night in the drying room will probably be insufficient time to dry out the inside. A rifle, with telescope sight attached, should not be put into a damp cover for there is a high risk of the moisture within the cover causing the 'scope to fog up (see page 39).

2

Telescope Sights

*Selection, use and care of – 'Scope used as a range
finder – Sighting-in a telescope sight*

(a) *Selection, use and care of*

Provided one's eyesight is good, the open sight for stalking Red
deer in Scotland, where weather conditions at times can be
extremely wet, is probably the best, but whether the sight
should be a combination of broad, flat or medium backsight
with a large or small bead foresight, or a narrow V backsight
with a thin blade or tiny bead foresight is a matter of individual
taste. Personally, I would always recommend a broad flat V
backsight – with a silver or ivory tipped foresight of medium
diameter – say about 1.6 mm. (1/16 in.).

With open sights, aiming requires that three points have to be
lined up – the near sight, the front bead and the aiming point on
the target. Youthful eyes can generally cope, but with ageing
eyesight the time will come when the majority of sportsmen find
that even with glasses, they can no longer focus sharply on these
three points, and if missed or wounded beasts are to be avoided,
an alternative sight has to be found.

Before the war, one alternative was the aperture or 'peep'
sight (Lyman Sight) which reduced the focal points from three
to two, and this was a great improvement over the open sight
and many sportsmen used it with considerable success in
Scotland.

The telescope sight ('scope) goes one better, for you only
have to sight your game in the field of the telescope, and there,
in the same focus, appearing at the same distance, is the
reticule, sharp and clear, indicating the exact point at which the
bullet will strike the target at the range for which the sight has
been zeroed.

Because of the difference in human eyes, 'scopes must be focusable to suit the individual and with proper focus, both target and reticule will have maximum sharpness. Focusing, therefore, is something which must be done by yourself. Most 'scopes, therefore, are provided for focusing with the eyepiece. Should you have to lend your rifle at any time to a friend, remember that the focus may have been altered to suit his eye, so that when the rifle is returned, the focus should be immediately checked.

Care must be taken, when crawling, to see that the 'scope does not get damaged against rocks, and when the shot is taken it must always be remembered that although the target can be clearly seen in the 'scope, the barrel, being some 3 to 4 cm. (about 1½ in.) lower, may be directed against a rock or bank.

In woodland stalking the telescope sight is essential, for it enables one to see when the target is clear of any twigs, rocks or tree trunks. It is invaluable in poor light, and when Roe stalking in the early morning or late evening, it will add almost an hour to your stalking time and enable shots to be taken which, with open sights, would have been impossible.

Nevertheless, if your rifle is fitted with an open sight – but not all rifles are today – it is as well to make yourself proficient with the open sight for the day may come when rain or fogging up, or perhaps an accident, will have rendered the 'scope useless, and unless stalking for the day is to be abandoned, the open sights will have to be used.

One of the main disadvantages of using a telescope sight in Scotland is that in some seasons more stalking days than not are wet ones, and to keep the glass dry is always a problem, not only from rain or mist, but also during a long crawl through wet rushes or heather. Keeping the rifle and 'scope within the rifle cover until the very last moment, together with tight-fitting lens caps, will undoubtedly help but should there be any delay in taking the shot once the cap has been removed, unless one has an inexhaustible supply of dry tissue to soak up the water on the lens, the 'scope will soon become useless. For just such an emergency I have always taken out a liberal supply of *loose* tissue sheets in a polythene bag which should keep them dry until they are actually withdrawn from the bag. It is next to useless, however, to take out a length of paper without first separating the individual sheets, for any attempt to do this on the hill in pouring rain and a gale force wind will soon leave you with a sodden lump of tissue, quite useless for the purpose for which it had been brought.

The lens cap straps should be secured to the body of the 'scope by a strap or adhesive tape and this will prevent them being lost whilst a shot is being taken.

Sometimes in wet weather I use part of an old Barbour jacket sleeve which is slipped over the rifle completely covering the 'scope. When the time comes to fire the rifle the sleeve can either be pulled down to the barrel end, or rolled up at each end so that vision through the 'scope is clear.

Rain, itself, does not normally cause internal fogging of a telescope sight for it generally occurs on the day *following* a very wet one on the hill, and is invariably caused by carrying the rifle and 'scope in a rifle case that had not completely dried out overnight. What has happened is that when a 'scope, which is not completely airtight, has been put into a damp rifle cover which is still warm from having been taken out of the drying cupboard, the air within the tube tries to expand, and there is an outward pressure. When the 'scope gets cold, as it will when taken out of the cover on the hill, the air within the tube will tend to condense the moisture of the air within the 'scope and 'fogging' is the result. Unless, therefore, there are drying facilities available that will dry out thoroughly both the outside and *inside* of your cover, it is essential to have two covers for the rifle, so that a completely dry one will always be available to start the day. Should fogging within the telescope sight start to appear on the hill, I did find, on one occasion, that if the 'scope was grasped tightly in the hand for perhaps ten to thirty minutes, dependent on the degree of fogging present, the warmth of the hand eventually dispelled it, and it gave me no further trouble that day.

The lens of the 'scope should, of course, be coated or

bloomed, as this will increase light transmission by almost 30 per cent compared to an uncoated lens.

There are a large number of 'scope mounts available. These include Parker-Hale, Sako, Redfield and various German mounts. Unless the 'scope and mount are integral and form one unit which cannot work loose, the 'scope should never be removed from the rifle for it will probably upset the zeroing. Furthermore, frequent removal of the 'scope must eventually cause some wear to the mounts, and accuracy will suffer.

Be careful to see that the 'scope is not mounted too close to the eye, otherwise on recoil, you are likely to finish up with a cut or bruising round the eye. Rifle stocks vary slightly in length but I would suggest that any distance less than 30.5 cm. (12 in.) between the butt-end and the eyepiece of the 'scope – which allows about 8.9 cm. (3½ in.) eye relief – is asking for trouble, particularly when taking a steep uphill prone shot. Some 'scopes have a rubber or neoprene ring around the eye-piece to reduce the blow should contact with the face be made on firing.

The cheek plays an important part in helping to hold the rifle steady, and when using open sights, the stock will – or should – fit comfortably against the cheek. When a telescope sight is fitted above the open sight, unless the head is raised about a couple of centimetres or so (say one to one-and-half inches) it will be impossible to see through the 'scope at all. The stock, therefore, is no longer a good fit with the cheek, and in consequence one has great difficulty in holding the rifle really steady.

The Germans have long appreciated this, and some of their rifles are provided with a rising cheek-piece which jumps into position on pressing a button, thus providing a good support for the shooter's cheek. I, personally, have made a small wooden attachment about 22 cm. (8½ in.) long which raises the cheek level by about 3 cm. (1¼ in.). This is held in position by means of two split pins, which enable it to be quickly clamped into position. The overall length of this attachment is really governed by the amount of room required to remove the rifle bolt, for it must not foul this mechanism. Unless one removes

2 Raising the height of the stock with a detachable cheek-piece provides better support when using a 'scope.

the attachment one cannot, of course, use the open sights as the head will be too high. The detachable cheek-piece has to be carefully planed down to suit the user's cheek – for few cheeks have a standard profile.

The 'scope should be mounted low on the rifle so that the line of sight is as near as possible to the line of bore and on most rifles it should be possible to do this within about 3 cm. (1¼ in.).

With a very low mounting, however, no provision can be made to use the open sight with the 'scope *in situ* as is possible with a 'scope mounted on stilts. Furthermore, with a low mounted telescope a faint 'ghost' of the foresight and foresight block can usually be seen in the lower half of the telescope.

A length of rubber tubing, attached to the front of the 'scope and projecting about 7 or 8 cm. (3 in.) can be helpful to shield out any sun glare on the front lens, whilst a similar piece of tubing, placed on the back of the 'scope between the eyepiece and your eye, will help to block out any side light on the eyepiece lens.

Telescope sights can be supplied with a variety of reticles, ranging from three broad posts to a fine hair line cross. In the accompanying sketch, which shows eight different types of reticle that can be fitted to 'scopes, whilst No. 1 is probably considered the standard type, I prefer No. 4 for it provides the combination of fine crosswires for precision shooting in good light, and stout posts to assist in shooting in the failing light of dawn or dusk.

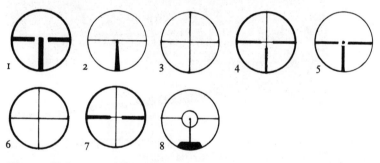

Figure 4 Telescope sight reticles

In any 'scope the field of view at near distance and at far distance is proportional. That is to say a field of view at 100 yards is exactly twice that width at 200 yards, or is one-half at 50 yards. Range-finder reticles are available from Weaver for some of their 'scopes. Similar to No. 3, this reticle has two horizontal cross-hairs instead of one, the space between them representing

6 in. (15.2 cm.) on the target at 100 yards, 12 in. (30.4 cm.) at 200 yards, etc.

(b) *'Scope used as range finder*

As a range guide the No. 4 reticle, with its space between the vertical and horizontal posts, is probably the best, and provided one has a rough idea of the body height of the deer, it is a simple matter to ascertain in the field what the distance between the horizontal posts represents when viewing a deer at ranges of 50, 100 and 200 yards, etc. (46, 91 and 183 metres).

Using a square (112 cm. × 112 cm.) to represent a Red deer stag, the body size will appear as in figure 5.

Using a smaller square (67.5 cm. × 67.5 cm.) to represent a Roe deer, the body size will appear as in figure 5.

A Range table, therefore, for all six species of deer, when viewed through a Nickel 4-power 'scope is as follows:

	Approx. body square size	(a) Body fills space between lateral pillars		(b) Body fills space between one lateral pillar and vertical line		(c) Body fills half space between one lateral pillar and fine vertical line	
	Centimetres	yards	metres	yards	metres	yards	metres
Red deer	112 × 112	125	114	250	228	500	456
Fallow deer	84 × 84	95	87	190	173	380	346
Sika deer	74 × 74	85	78	170	155	340	310
Roe deer	68 × 68	75	69	150	137	300	274
Muntjac	52 × 52	62	57	124	113	248	226
Chinese Water-deer	52 × 52	62	57	124	113	248	226

Note: The body size of the deer will vary, of course, according to magnification of the 'scope, so the above figures only apply to a 4-power 'scope.

For Red and Roe deer, see figures 6 (p. 45) and 7 (p. 46) respectively.

Whenever a deer is shot it is good practice to first estimate the range, and then pace it out to see how accurate your estimation

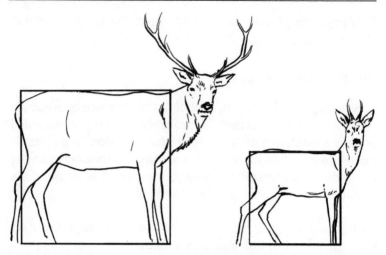

Figure 5 The body of a deer, excluding head and neck, is almost a square. Thus a piece of board 112 cm. × 112 cm. (44 in. × 44 in.) would represent a Scottish Red deer stag, whilst a smaller piece 67.5 cm. × 67.5 cm. (27 in. × 27 in.) a Roe buck.

has been. I generally find that stalkers are inclined to under, rather than over, estimate range, but whether this is always done purposefully to assure the 'rifle' that the shot is not as difficult as he appears to think, I cannot say. On a few occasions I am sure it is, however.

When shooting with a telescope sight concentrate your attention on the part of the deer being aimed at rather than on the cross-wires of the 'scope, the theory being that what your eye is focused on will automatically be followed by the line of sight through the 'scope. On the other hand, concentration on the cross-wires against a 'deer background' may fail, until too late, to pick up any slight movement on the part of the deer which will result in a misplaced shot. In other words, focus on the deer *through* the 'scope rather than looking 'close-up' at the reticles *in* the 'scope.

A recent development in the design of some sporting 'scopes is to have the eyepiece rectangular rather than circular in shape but whether this is an improvement, I cannot say.

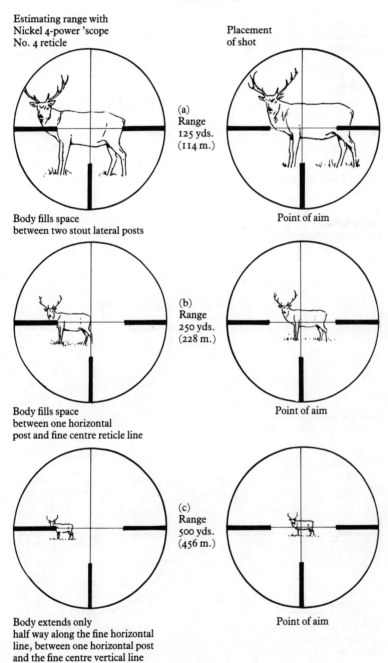

Estimating range with
Nickel 4-power 'scope
No. 4 reticle

Placement
of shot

(a)
Range
125 yds.
(114 m.)

Body fills space
between two stout lateral posts

Point of aim

(b)
Range
250 yds.
(228 m.)

Body fills space
between one horizontal
post and fine centre reticle line

Point of aim

(c)
Range
500 yds.
(456 m.)

Body extends only
half way along the fine horizontal
line, between one horizontal post
and the fine centre vertical line

Point of aim

Figure 6 Using a 'scope as a range finder – Red deer.

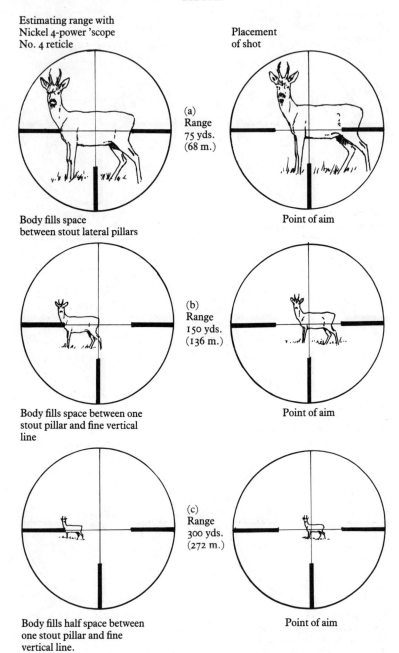

Estimating range with
Nickel 4-power 'scope
No. 4 reticle

Placement
of shot

(a)
Range
75 yds.
(68 m.)

Body fills space
between stout lateral pillars

Point of aim

(b)
Range
150 yds.
(136 m.)

Body fills space between one
stout pillar and fine vertical
line

Point of aim

(c)
Range
300 yds.
(272 m.)

Body fills half space between
one stout pillar and fine
vertical line.

Point of aim

Figure 7 Using a 'scope as a range finder – Roe deer.

It will be appreciated that the telescope sight is a fairly delicate instrument, and should be treated with care. It should never be used as a convenient handle for carrying the rifle, though I have seen a number of people doing just this. It is a modern aid that not only prolongs the stalking days for the fit sportsman whose eyesight is, perhaps, failing but also helps to make the sport of stalking more humane. It should never be a means to encourage lazy stalking by long-range shooting.

If you have to wear glasses for stalking, keep them clean, particularly the upper half which is the part used when viewing through a 'scope sight.

Before closing mention should be made of the Single Point Sight which was introduced for use with rifle or gun a number of years ago by the Normark Corporation of Minnesota, USA. This weighs 8½ oz. (.241 kilos) and is mounted on similar mounts to a normal telescope sight. This sight is not a precision one for shooting at a stationary target and as such should not be considered for hill or woodland stalking. It is certainly a sight for shooting running game, and would, therefore, perhaps come into its own at a continental boar drive, but not on deer in the United Kingdom.

(c) *Sighting-in a telescope sight*

If you should have acquired a new telescope sight for your rifle, or due to some accident, find the sight has gone out of alignment, it is a simple matter to zero the rifle, and you must do this yourself for no two people shoot exactly alike.

First rest the rifle on a sandbag or other suitable support – a vice would be best of all – and after removing the bolt, take a sight through the bore on a target such as a small white one-inch (2.5 cm.) square placed on a black bull's eye, set at about 100 yards (91 metres) distance. After securing the rifle *steady* on the bull as sighted through the bore, without moving the rifle *at all*, look through the telescope sight, and if the reticles are not crossing the centre of the bull, adjustment will have to be made to bring the reticles on to the bull.

Before making any adjustments, however, it is essential to know which way to turn the adjustment screws. With American or Japanese 'scopes this offers no problem for when the caps are unscrewed, a graduated dial is revealed with an arrow pointing 'L' indicating Left, for horizontal adjustment, and 'U' or 'H' indicating 'Up' or 'High' for vertical adjustment. With German and Austrian 'scopes, the graduated dials are marked 'Auf/Ab' (up/down) and 'RE/LI' (Right/Left).

With a little practice it should be possible to get the reticles lined up relative to the bore to within about 1½ in. (4 cm.) at 100 yards (91 metres).

The rifle is now ready for testing on the range, and although the first shots will not necessarily cut the bull, they should at least be within about 2 inches (5 cm.) of it, and any further adjustment necessary can be made with the minimum expenditure of ammunition. Until you have had some practice in sighting-in a rifle, it is useful to place a large piece of cardboard about 2 ft. square (60 cm. square) immediately behind the target, and this will indicate any wild shooting should the initial shots have missed the bull entirely. Make a note of the number of clicks required to bring a bullet strike, say, 2 in. (5 cm.) off centre to the centre of the bull. Unfortunately, not all makes of telescopes have the same adjustment, and whilst it may take, when zeroing at 100 yards, six clicks on an Austrian or German telescope to make this correction, with an American or Japanese 'scope up to 8 clicks may be required. Some 'scopes such as the Stirling Bisley De Luxe indicate on the adjustment screw dial that one tick represents ¼ in. (0.6 cm.) movement on target at 100 yards (91 metres), which is very helpful.

The majority of telescope sights have a small numbered dial and locking grub screw fitted to the top of the sight adjustment screws, and when zeroed the dial should be locked with the number '0' opposite the arrow, and this will act as a guide for any subsequent adjustment.

If you own a rifle such as a .30-06 or .270 Winchester for which a range of bullet weights are available, although you may normally use only one weight of bullet, say the 150 gr., for all deer shooting in this country, the opportunity may occur for boar or elk shooting in Europe for which it would be advisable to use a heavier bullet – say 220 gr. – but before doing so in the field, the rifle will have to be zeroed. Make a careful note of the number of clicks required to place the 220 gr. bullet at the same spot on the target as the 150 gr. at the same range. Then, when you wish to resume using the lighter bullet, all that is required is to adjust the horizontal reticle by the same number of clicks by which it had been altered for the heavier bullet.

For instance, zeroing at 100 yards, an adjustment of 4 clicks is required on the Nickel Vari-power 'scope fitted to my .30-06 rifle when changing from the 220 gr. to 150 gr. bullet (Winchester Super X) and a note of this is made on the cartridge carton. Some shooters when required to make an adjustment of, say, 4 clicks, prefer to turn the adjustment screw 5 clicks, and then reverse 1 click, in the belief that the result may be more precise.

Should at any time on the hill or in the forest the telescope sight be subjected to a severe knock, it is always a wise precaution to check the zeroing and, having unloaded and withdrawn the bolt this can be roughly done through the bore as described on page 47 with the top of a telegraph pole, tree stump or other prominent spot as a target. If it appears that the zeroing of the rifle has been seriously affected by the fall, it is best to abandon any further stalking until the rifle has been properly zeroed on the range, for any misplaced shot in consequence may result in a wounded beast. Furthermore, much shooting that may be required to sight-in the rifle on the hill is not to be recommended, for it is bound to cause some disturbance.

A device called a Scope Aligner has recently been put on the market by Parker-Hale. It is claimed that this makes a telescope sight and rifle barrel align perfectly without a shot being fired, but I have not had the opportunity to test this equipment.

I have yet to find a rifle, fitted with even the best of telescope sights, that does not need the zeroing checked from time to time. If you are confident in your rifle – *and* in your shooting ability – you will soon know when the sight is not shooting true.

You don't have to have a miss to tell you this, for a series of badly placed shots will inform you that your shots are not hitting the point of aim, and you should, therefore, have the zeroing checked.

Throughout the book it will be noted that I have referred to 'Telescope Sights' rather than 'Telescopic Sights', for I consider that the latter should refer to an instrument in which some parts are telescopic, i.e. capable of being pushed in or pulled out, such as the legs of a telescopic tripod. According to the *Oxford English Dictionary*, a telescope is an instrument for 'making distant objects appear nearer and larger' – which is precisely what a 'scope sight achieves.

3

Equipment and Miscellaneous

Binoculars or Telescope – Clothing – Knives – Sticks –
Check-list of equipment for the hill or woodland stalker

(a) *Binoculars or telescope*

Fifty years ago, anyone who regularly stalked the Scottish Red
deer used a telescope but since the war, the 'long glass' has
gradually been replaced by modern high-power binoculars
which are not only easier to use, but stand up better to wet
weather. For the older generation of professional stalkers in
Scotland, however, the telescope is still first choice.

An advantage of binoculars over the telescope is that not only
is focusing easier, but a much larger field of country is covered,
thus making it easier to pick up deer at a reasonable distance.
Once having found them, however, unless the range is comparatively short, it will be almost impossible, without a closer
approach, to judge whether any beast in the herd is worth a
stalk.

The telescope, on the other hand, by virtue of its greater
magnification, can save many miles of walking after a deer
which, on close inspection, is found to be unshootable. Spying
through a telescope is far less tiring on the eyes than with
binoculars, particularly those above $8\times$ magnification, which in
a very short time seem to 'draw' the eyes.

One of the disadvantages of the telescope, however, is that
when in close proximity to deer, it is an unwieldy piece of
equipment to keep taking out in order to confirm that the
position of the selected beast has not changed during the stalk.
In order to overcome this, some stalkers take out binoculars as
well as the telescope and this is certainly ideal, the main
drawback being that it involves another piece of equipment
slung around the neck. Zeiss, however, make a small 8×20

binoculars which weigh only 170 gm. (just over 5¾ oz.) whilst an alternative to binoculars for this close-up work could be a monocular such as the Wray 8 × 21 which is even lighter, weighing only 114 gm. (4 oz.). Both the Zeiss and the Wray can easily be carried in a breast pocket and of the two, on price alone, the monocular is preferable. Whichever you select, it should always be attached by a cord or leather bootlace to the buttonhole in your coat lapel, otherwise it will soon be lost.

In damp, wet or misty weather telescopes fog up very easily, and once this happens, no matter how many times the lenses are mopped up, they soon fog up again.

If lenses have to be removed for drying or cleaning, care must be taken not to strip the thread when reassembling. A light, anti-clockwise turn before attempting to screw clockwise is often helpful in engaging the correct thread. A fogged-up or damp telescope should be dried out in a warm room and, with the draws pulled out to their extremities, left overnight on a mantelpiece or shelf. Never put a telescope in the direct heat of a fire but let it dry out gradually. On wet days a waterproof sleeve or cover can be slipped over the telescope whilst it is being used for spying, and this will help, for a time, in keeping out the wet, and is certainly worth trying. Some people use a dressing of vaseline on the 'draws' as a protection against wet. The best advice on wet days, however, is that if two of you are out each with a telescope, only one should be used until that becomes useless, and the second one can then be put in commission – for it is pointless fogging up both glasses together.

The amount of magnification required in a telescope for deer stalking is a matter of personal choice, bearing in mind that the higher the magnification the less will be the area of ground covered by the 'glass', and the greater in consequence will be the task of finding the deer. Once deer have been found, however, the 'glass' of higher magnification will obviously tell you more about them – such as the number of points on the antlers, age or sex. For Scottish stalking a telescope of about 18 or 24 magnification is probably best.

Weight, too, is important, for a telescope has to be carried throughout many hours of tramping the hills, and although one made of an aluminium alloy will be about half the weight of one made of brass (about 1.5 kg. or 3⅓ lb.), there is no doubt that the latter will stand up to far harder use than the alloy ones, which need fairly careful handling on rocky ground, otherwise they can be easily dented and as a result will not draw out properly. Nevertheless, if a lightweight telescope is required, it is well worth looking out for a good, second-hand three-draw telescope made in these lightweight alloys, for their weight is only about 0.8 kg. (1¾ lb.) to which a further 0.22 kg. (½ lb.) should be added for a leather case, which must be strong and reinforced to prevent it being squashed and so damaging the telescope within. Some people dispense with a leather case, using leather caps only, which are held together by a strap, for the protection of the two ends. This, however, is not good enough for stalking for the body of the telescope itself, particularly those made of lightweight alloy, need just as much protection as the ends, and in wet weather the entire telescope needs protection. It is a good thing to have one's initials on the case – and perhaps on the telescope itself – for many telescopes look alike! It will also help the stalker to return the correct one should it have been taken away overnight for drying.

Always replace the telescope in the case after each spy, and remember to buckle the straps. Failure to do this may result in its loss – or at best – much time lost in trying to recover it.

A few stalkers who rely on binoculars to find the deer, instead of a conventional three-draw telescope, take out one of the modern Spotting Scopes, which can be either hand held or used with a small tripod mounting. Weights vary from one make to another, the Bushnell rubber-armoured 50 mm. prismatic scope, which has a length of 34 cm. (13¼ in.) weighing about 1 kg. (35 oz.).

In woodland stalking, where ranges generally are short, there is no doubt that binoculars are best, for the greater field of vision offered by them is a big advantage in thick cover.

With binoculars it is best to keep off those of very high

magnification, for not only are they hard to keep steady without some elbow support, but as already mentioned, they are a strain on the eyes. Binoculars, therefore, of 7 × 40 (or 50) or 8 × 40 (or 50) would seem to be about the best for woodland stalking, the 7 × or 8 × signifying magnification and indicating that the subject is viewed 7 or 8 times its normal size. The '40' or '50' indicates that the object glass (OG) which influences the brilliance of the picture, and the field of view, is 40 or 50 mm. in diameter. Thus binoculars 7 × 50 would give a brighter image than one marked 7 × 30, and would normally cost more.

Binoculars, apart from the mini-models such as the Zeiss 8 × 20 already mentioned, vary in weight from about 566 gm. (18 oz.) to about 1½ kg. (3¼ lb.) according to manufacture and magnification. Ex WD naval binoculars, however, could weigh considerably more.

Recently I have been trying out a Falcon 7-21 × 40 zoom binoculars, and when the optics have been improved, this undoubtedly will be the glass of the future for it is able to combine at 7 × 40 the advantages of medium power binoculars with, at 21 × 40 the magnification of a medium power telescope. Light gathering in the higher magnification ranges, however, leaves a lot to be desired in the half light of dawn and dusk which is the time they will be most used by the roe-stalker. For hill stalking, however, during the middle part of the day, provided the light is reasonably good and there is good support for the elbows to ensure steady focusing, I found them at 21 × 40 adequate to identify individual stags at ranges at which, with 7 × 40 binoculars, they would have been unrecognisable. Depth of focus at high power is extremely fine, and even at low power one cannot get sharp focus on objects closer than about 18 metres (20 yards). The focusing, by means of a hinged lever instead of the usual screw, was, however, the best I have yet seen on any binoculars, and is extremely good for making any adjustment with gloved hands during wintry weather. Zoom adjustment is also by lever. Zoom binoculars with similar focusing arrangements are also produced by Bushnell (Bausch and Lomb).

In hill stalking, binoculars will generally be carried in a case to keep them dry, and only taken out for spying, or hung around the neck during the final stages of a stalk when repeated spying will be required. In woodland stalking, however, the binoculars must be available at all times for instant and immediate spying, and so will be carried slung around the neck, and the case, therefore, will probably be left in the car. There should, however, be some protection in rainy weather for the eyepieces, and whilst some binoculars are provided with a special cover for this purpose, for those without, a suitable cover can be made by attaching to the neck strap a flap of leather or rubber which can be dropped out of the way when viewing. Many binoculars, particularly of Japanese origin, are supplied with two separate plastic covers for the eyepieces, but these are quite useless and soon get lost. The cover for the eyepieces must be in one unit.

Binoculars used for military purposes often contain a scale in the right eyepiece. This is known as a graticule and is used to estimate distances, or when the distance is known, the size of an object viewed. Habicht are prepared to incorporate a scale in binoculars required for hunting on request.

Whatever make is selected to supplement the telescope on the hill, it is pointless to take out binoculars costing several hundred pounds, when a Japanese make of similar 'advertised optics' costing under £100 can do the job almost as well and will not incur any great financial hardship if lost or damaged. For woodland stalking, however, you get what you pay for, and the best quality you can afford will be an investment. The disadvantage of many of the cheaper binoculars is that sharp focus cannot be obtained on close-in subjects – which, of course, is essential when stalking in thick cover. In other words, therefore, the sedentary stalker who shoots most of his deer from a 'High-seat' should buy the best he can afford, but for the young and active, one of the cheaper Japanese models is probably adequate.

The difference between using a telescope or a pair of medium power binoculars is that, whilst the latter can be used quite adequately when standing without any elbow support, it is

3 Spying with telescope, in sitting position, using stick for support.

4 Spying with telescope in standing position, using stick for support against the body.

essential that some support is available when using the telescope. The best and easiest way to use a telescope is to sit down,
choosing, if possible, a fairly dry place, with a good backrest
and by raising the left (or right) knee, use this as a support for
the arm holding the telescope, whilst the other hand grasping
the eyepiece close to the face, is used for adjusting the focus. A
stick in the ground alongside the bent knee can also be used as
an additional or alternative support to the knee, and if a stick is
not carried, the rifle can be used – barrel-end uppermost of
course! If you are sitting, unless some support such as a bank or
rock can be found for the head, the neck will soon start to ache if
the session of spying is at all prolonged. At times, however, it
may be advantageous to take a quick spy whilst standing –
perhaps to have another look at some distant deer being stalked,
or others that may have just come into view round the shoulder
of a hill – and if the end of the stick is rested against the
abdomen instead of being stuck in the ground as when sitting, a
fair means of support is obtained.

As to the correct manner in which the ground should be
spied, whether with telescope or binoculars, but in particular
with the former, this should be done in a succession of vertical

Figure 8 Spy the ground in vertical rather than horizontal sweeps.

rather than lateral sweeps of the glass, for by the latter method small bits of ground can so easily be overlooked. By vertical sweeps one can slide the hand supporting the telescope very slowly down the stick, having started at a fixed point on the skyline, and working the glass slowly downwards until the ground, perhaps some 200 to 400 metres (about 220 to 440 yards) in front of you, is reached. The telescope is then worked slowly back to the skyline on a course which should *just* include the ground on the extreme left or right side (dependent on whether you are spying the ground from right to left or vice versa) of your previous vertical sweep. When the skyline is reached the whole process is repeated downwards and upwards again until the whole piece of ground to be spied has been covered. Some stalkers prefer to spy the ground in horizontal sweeps, but the main disadvantage of this method is that unless the horizontal sweeps are restricted to very short distances, one's body position is continually having to be shifted, first to the left and then to the right as more and more ground is covered. Moreover in lateral sweeps, one is apt to follow ground contours instead of keeping strictly to the horizontal, and in consequence small pieces of ground can so easily be overlooked.

When deer are spotted, study the surrounding ground *very* carefully through the glass *before* trying to see the deer with the naked eye, trying, if possible, to pick out some prominent landmark such as a big rock, rowan tree, waterfall etc. as a guide to their whereabouts. Normally one eye will be closed when using the telescope but it is useful when deer have been spotted through the glass to open the other eye, for this will give you the general direction in which the deer are located. The spying eye can also be temporarily closed as this may assist some people to see through the free eye, but if this is done it is essential that the telescope should remain on the deer, otherwise there may be some difficulty in relocating them.

In sunny weather be sure that the lens hood is fully extended, otherwise the rays of the sun may be reflected off the lens, and nothing is more likely to catch the eye of a deer than a flashing light on the hillside. Even the body of the telescope – particularly the older types made of brass or those with the blacking worn off the 'draws' – will reflect the sun's rays.

Practice makes perfect, and never was this truer than in the use of a telescope and even though your stalking holiday may last for only two or three weeks in the year, this needn't limit the use of the telescope to that short period alone. Birds, boats at sea, and even aeroplanes, are all good 'targets' to practise on. Don't be content until the 'glass' can be used equally well with either eye, for it is useful, during a long bout of spying, to be able to rest each eye in turn – particularly the eye which will eventually be used when firing the shot. Remember, also, that the spy is the introduction to the stalk, and even when a shootable beast has been found, make sure before putting the glass away, that other deer are not going to interfere with the approach.

(b) *Clothing and footwear*

Footwear is a matter of personal choice, and whereas in pre-war days well nailed leather boots were invariably worn by the highland deer stalker, today leather has largely been replaced by rubber, and the short rubber ankle length boot is much in evidence. Spats or short puttees are useful in preventing snow and wet heather seeds going down the top of the boots.

In former days, however, the Scottish deer stalker had to walk considerably longer distances than his modern counterpart to both shoot and retrieve his deer, but mechanised transport has now made many a far beat more accessible, and the main concern of some sportsmen in selecting their footwear for the hill is not its ability to withstand abrasive action of many miles of foot slogging, but whether he can come home with dry feet. As a result, some sportsmen are now able to dismount from their wheeltrack vehicle attired in tight fitting rubber knee length boots more suitable for a flight pond in East Anglia than for a long walk or climb in the Scottish mountains.

The short rubber ankle boots, which should be a size larger than normally taken so as to allow an extra pair of socks to be worn, are also ideal for woodland stalking, and when conditions underfoot in summer or early autumn are extremely dry, rubber soled canvas shoes or even tennis shoes are the best. The main thing in footwear for the woods is lightness, and a thin sole so that the wearer can detect any twigs in his path and so avoid snapping them. The conventional rubber knee length boot, however, should be avoided, not only because its very design makes silent walking almost an impossibility, but also the scraping of branches and undergrowth against the leg of the boot cannot fail to announce your approach to the deer.

Whatever type of footwear you select, always have a second pair available so that you can at least start the day dry shod. If the boots have laces, make sure they are sound and replace them whenever fraying starts to appear. A small stock of laces should, therefore, always be available.

On the continent the majority of professional hunters or *jägers* wear an official uniform which looks extremely smart and whilst in former times many of the larger estates in Scotland used to provide their stalkers and ghillies with a suit made with cloth to match the official tweed or tartan of the house, this practice has largely disappeared, and the dress of most stalkers is generally similar to that worn by the 'gentleman', the main difference being that the latter is often far more shabbily dressed than the professional man!

Almost any old clothing will do, but should it be new, a few weeks crawling in the mountains will soon see that it will not remain so for long! The colour should be one that will blend into the hillside. For this reason it may be an advantage to have a jacket of different shade to the trousers – say a reddish brown jacket with a darker brown for the trousers. Colours of a Lovat mixture, however, are inclined to show up black when wet and are not, therefore, recommended.

A commando-type camouflage jacket is also a useful garment, for in addition to being wind and shower proof, it is not too noisy when crawling. Not all camouflage jackets for sale today, however, are up to WD quality for there are lots of substandard jackets available which should be avoided.

For the hill, plus-four trousers are undoubtedly better than close fitting knee breeches, for no matter how wet they become, the baggy part around the knees, once it stops raining, will soon dry out in the wind, and even when wet are not too uncomfortable provided the tailor has not been skimpy with the cloth, to enable them to hang mostly clear of the knees. Tight-fitting knee breeches, however, once wet, will remain uncomfortably clammy around the knees for a very long time and eventually may encourage rheumatism in later years. Jeans are definitely out.

For woodland stalking a plus-four suit is also good, particularly if made of green loden cloth which makes it the most silent of all material for moving around in undergrowth. Unfortunately the weave of loden cloth is unsuitable for any prolonged crawling on the hill.

During the summer and early autumn, when the midges are about, it may be advisable to replace plus-fours with conventional trousers, for these winged pests, despite copious amounts of insect repellent, seem to delight in homing in on stocking-covered legs!

In the old days it was considered a trifle 'cissy' to wear a raincoat on the hill, the stalkers relying on their tweeds to keep their backs dry for at least the first hour or so of the day. Today, however, opinions have changed and a raincoat is often part of a stalker's equipment.

What type of coat is worn is a matter of personal choice, but it should certainly not be one made from plastic or rubberised cloth, for although both are good rain repellents, they also retain body perspiration and the wearer may finish up as wet as though no coat had been worn at all. For hill stalking, the coat should be short enough to leave the knees free when crawling.

A waterproof extension flap fitted to the back of the jacket can be very useful for sitting on whilst spying or resting on damp ground. When not in use the flap is buttoned up out of the way. This is far better than carrying a small waterproof sheet about in a pocket for sitting on in wet places, as some people do. The Roe sack can also be used to provide a dry seat, or the waterproof liner wrapped over the knees to keep them dry whilst sitting in a 'High-seat' during rain.

When not being worn the coat can be carried in a game bag slung over the shoulder, and if the bag itself is secured to the waist with a light strap, this will prevent it slipping around whilst crawling. The bag and coat can also serve as a useful rest for the rifle when the shot is being taken (see page 111). A rucksack, or Roe-carrying bag, is not suitable for this purpose on the hill, for when crawling, like a snail's shell on your back, it becomes too visible.

Waterproof leggings should never be worn for stalking for not only are they uncomfortably hot but they make a horrible swishing noise, particularly when crawling. A raincoat can also be extremely noisy when crawling flat out *ventre à terre*, but the majority of crawls are generally executed on hands and knees thus reducing contact of the coat on the ground to a minimum.

One of the reasons for reluctance in former days to wearing a raincoat was this noise problem, and with open sights shots were seldom taken at ranges beyond 100 metres, so the stalking party was often nearer to their target than today, and this increased the risk of the deer hearing their approach.

A friend of mine solves this problem by wearing an old oversize tweed jacket *over* his Barbour coat, and this, of course, allows him to crawl silently through the heather etc.

The one occasion when I do put on leggings is when I am stalking Sika deer and have to crawl across a meadow that has recently been visited by the 'muck-spreader', and on grass, particularly when wet, as distinct from heather and rushes, I find crawling in leggings is not unduly noisy. It is, however, nice for all concerned to be able to discard one's 'crawlers' on completion of the stalk without bringing the farmyard smells into the car or house!

Barbour leggings and jackets, particularly when old and treated with thornproof dressing, are more pliable than the new garment, and in consequence less noisy to wear. Rubberised waterproofs are undoubtedly the worst in this respect.

In woodland stalking, unless sitting in a 'High-seat', a rain-coat should not be worn, for no matter how carefully you walk, it is quite impossible to move silently without the occasional brush of the coat against a twig or bush. For a damp vigil in a 'High-seat', however, provided one doesn't fidget about too much, waterproof trousers are acceptable. For woodland stalk-ing, however, a loden cape is ideal, for not only is the garment completely silent but it is also almost waterproof, and when worn over the shoulders, is able to provide good protection against the rain for rifle and 'scope until the moment of shooting.

The cap should be of the 'deer-stalker' type with peak back and front to prevent the rain going down one's neck. In wet weather a short scarf made of towelling can be very useful in helping to soak up any excess water reaching the neck region. Even in fine weather, it is advisable to take out a woollen scarf, for weather and temperature on the hill can change rapidly and when not needed it can easily be slipped into a pocket.

With regard to pockets, I always have two inner 'hare-pockets' included in each side of my jacket, for these large pockets are extremely useful for carrying such things as scarves, spare gloves or sandwiches etc. Pockets – preferably fitted with a flap – should be capable of buttoning up so as to prevent the contents falling out during a crawl.

When hind stalking in cold weather those little lighter-fluid hand warmers can be very useful and should be included in the equipment of the winter stalker. When there is snow on the ground, for better camouflage a white smock complete with hood is useful to slip over the jacket. An old white sheet, with a hole cut in it and worn poncho fashion, will suffice. Some stalkers wear a white boiler type suit made of PVC type material. Although light and reasonably silent when moving, its main drawback is the lack of air within the garment, and this promotes excessive sweating. Woollen gloves or a pair of waterproof mittens, with complete cover for all fingers except for a flap to permit access to the rifle trigger when shooting, are very useful when the weather is really cold, but whether the latter are available in this country I am not sure. Mine, which I acquired whilst hunting in Montana, are filled with duck down for extra warmth. Even in summer or early autumn, outings at dawn or dusk can turn chilly at times, and it is wise, therefore, to always have a lightweight pair of mittens with you, not only for warmth when required, but also to provide some camouflage for pale hands which are subject to a certain amount of movement focusing binoculars or manipulating a Roe call.

What is worn beneath the jacket and trousers is again very much a personal matter dictated by the temperature and season of the year. Wool is undoubtedly the warmest for underwear, but there are people who cannot stand it next to the skin and prefer cotton, silk or a man-made fibre. My choice is unquestionably the first mentioned. For additional warmth a woollen sweater, preferably with polo neck, if not actually worn, could be slipped into the game bag along with the coat, or carried in the hare pocket. In cold weather when responding to a call of nature, a belt's buckle is easier to manipulate with frozen fingers than braces.

(c) *Knives*

After a deer has been shot, it will have to be gralloched and bled as soon as possible, and even if you yourself will not be required to gralloch the beast, a knife should, nevertheless, be part of your stalking equipment for knives can so easily be left at home or lost on the hill, and the professional stalker is no more immune to such happenings than you or I, so yours may have to be borrowed. There are other uses, also, besides gutting stags for which a knife can be useful at times, such as when Roe stalking, to remove one or two offending twigs in front of the 'High-seat' or even peeling an apple, so never be without one when stalking.

The blade should have a sharp, pointed end and be at least 7.6

cm. (3 in.) long – better still 12.7 cm. (5 in.). If it is of the folding type, it *must* have a good locking mechanism for the blade when extended – otherwise it can be a dangerous weapon particularly when bleeding a deer. Keep the blade sharp and clean, especially after gralloching a beast. It is quite useful to have a ring on the knife to which a cord can be attached. The other end of the cord, which should be about 90 cm. (3 ft.) in length, can be attached to a button-hole on your jacket, and this will prevent the knife being mislaid after a gralloch, or being lost during a crawl.

(d) *Sticks*

The majority of deer stalkers take a stick to the hill, for besides acting as a walking stick it can serve other useful purposes, such as a support for the telescope when spying, or as assistance when dragging a stag out of rough ground (see page 142). When used for the latter purpose, if the dragging ropes are wrapped round the stick, it will be found that grasping and pulling on the stick rather than the ropes will be much easier on the hands.

For woodland stalking a longer stick is required, and this should be no shorter than about 15 cm. (6 in.) less than the height of the user (see page 117). It must be rigid, and made, preferably, from ash or hazel. On the continent woodland stalkers often have two or three lightweight sticks loosely bound together at one end with a stout rubber band or leather thong, which can be used as a high tripod, thus affording more firm support than a single stick.

If the stick is metal shod at the end, be careful that it doesn't knock against a rock during a stalk, otherwise the deer will interpret its message and be off. A ring of deer antler is a better substitute for metal, otherwise have the stick unshod, and when it gets worn, replace it.

In 'still-hunting', when progress has to be *extremely* slow, a stick is very helpful to maintain one's balance when descending any steep or rough ground. It is also very useful in providing a 'third foot' when you are forced to freeze for a minute or two in the middle of a stride when 'still hunting'. Therefore, it is better to take short rather than long strides.

When searching for a shot deer in high bracken or grass a stick can be very useful for parting the foliage in front as you proceed.

When surmounting a barbed wire fence, lay a stick along the top strand of wire, it will prevent the barbs from catching on your trouser seat or legs.

Carrying a stick is not a sign of senility but common sense, and in woodland stalking it is a necessity.

(e) *Check-list for the hill or woodland stalker*

Most handbooks on stalking contain a check-list of items which the author considers essential for the stalker to take out with him, and I make no apologies for including my own list even though it must, of necessity, duplicate many of the items that have appeared in previous lists. Some of the items are only required by a stalker working on his own.

Hill stalking

Rifle
Ammunition (10–20 rounds)
Rifle cover
Telescope and/or binoculars or monocular
Stick
Knife
Whistle
Waterproof jacket★
Scarf★
Gloves and/or mittens
Stalker's hat
Insect repellent (autumn only)
Tissue sheets in polythene bag (for drying out 'scope etc.)
Lunch★
Compass (if on your own)
Game bag for carrying items marked ★

Woodland stalking

Rifle
Ammunition (10 rounds)
Binoculars
Stick – minimum length 150 cm. (5 ft.)
Knife
Whistle
Raincoat or cape†
Scarf
Gloves and/or mittens
Stalker's hat
Insect repellent (summer and autumn)†
Tissue sheets in polythene bag (for drying out 'scope etc.)
Roe-carrying sack
Roe calls (July and August)
Torch (evening outings)†
Boots (short rubber)

Hill stalking

Boots
Puttees (if required for boots)
Short socks (for rubber boots if worn)
Light rope – length 3 metres (about 10 ft.) if dragging necessary
Plastic survival bag* (winter hind shooting)
Elastoplast pieces

*Items to be carried in game bag.

Woodland stalking

Short socks (for wearing with boots)
Trailing line for dog†
Lengths of binder cord†
Elastoplast pieces†
Pruning saw (invaluable for removing twigs, etc. near 'High-seats' or on paths)
Tweezers (remove thorns, ticks etc.)
Small stainless steel mirror (to assist removal of foreign bodies from eye)

†Items to be carried in pocket or Roe-carrying sack.

Hill stalking
  Leave in car

Camera
Thermos (tea or coffee)
Spare box ammunition
Extra sweater
Whisky flask
Meat saw (if any necessity to cut up carcase on hill)
Dry socks ⎫ To drive home in, if
Shoes ⎭ long distance involved
Boards to help load carcase into car
Polythene bags
Towel (for drying rifle and 'scope)

Woodland stalking
  Leave in car

Camera
Lunch
Thermos (tea or coffee)
Binocular case
Spare box ammunition
Meat saw
Rifle cover
Saw ⎫ Required when
Nails (various) ⎬ erecting 'High
 ⎭ seats'
Dry socks ⎫ To drive home in, if
Shoes ⎭ long distance involved
Polythene bags
Towel for dog
Towel for drying rifle and 'scope
Dog – if not accompanying you on outing in wood

4

What to Shoot and How Many

Red deer – Roe deer – Other species – Ageing deer by
dental development and wear – (Red deer, Roe deer,
Other species)

The young stalker, keen to get blood on his knife and a trophy for his wall, will be anxious to shoot the first deer he happens to see. This is only natural, but when the first flush of success is over, the sooner he can learn what animals to shoot the better. Unfortunately this is something which cannot be acquired overnight, and even after years of conscientious stalking, errors will continue to be made. However, the price of knowledge is to make errors, and one should profit by mistakes.

First of all the stalker will have to know approximately how many deer of each sex should be killed on his ground.

In an ideally constituted deer population, the sex ratio should be about 1:1 of *all* age groups, and over the years the sex ratio of the calf or fawn increment will average out at 1:1. He should, therefore, try to achieve this balance.

(a) *Red deer*

In English woodland habitat the majority of hinds reach puberty as yearlings, having their first calf at two years of age, and will breed every year thereafter until about twelve. Under these conditions the annual number of calves from 100 hinds of all ages should be around 70, roughly divided between the sexes.

In the Scottish highlands, however, it is exceptional for a hind to have its first calf at under three years of age and accordingly the calf increment per 100 hinds will be reduced from about 70 to about 40 to 45. Twins are rare.

Ideally, if the March population both as regards numbers and

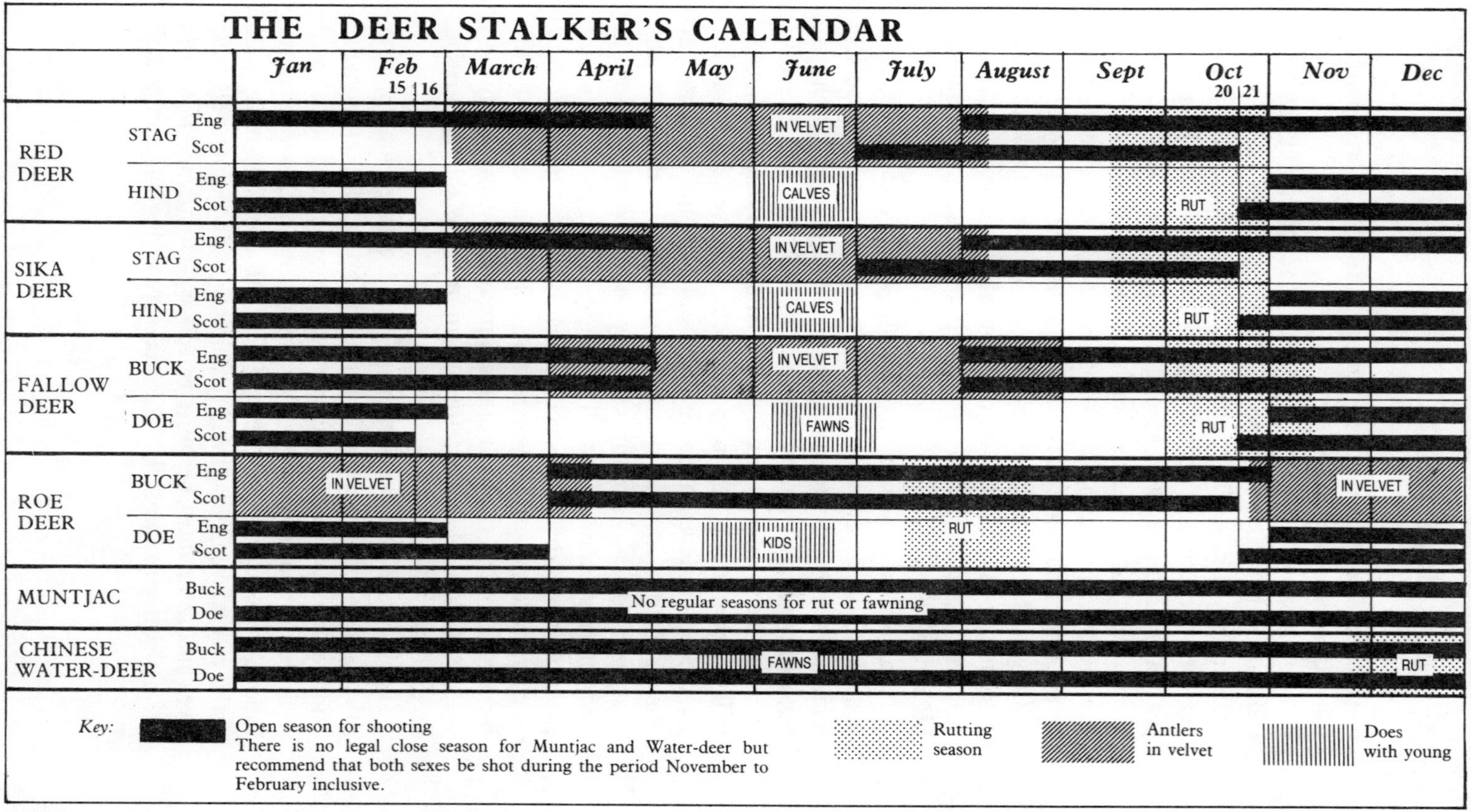
THE DEER STALKER'S CALENDAR
Jan
Feb
15 | 16
March
April
May
June
July
August
Sept
Oct
20 | 21
Nov
Dec
RED DEER
STAG
Eng
Scot
HIND
Eng
Scot
IN VELVET
CALVES
RUT
SIKA DEER
STAG
Eng
Scot
HIND
Eng
Scot
IN VELVET
CALVES
RUT
FALLOW DEER
BUCK
Eng
Scot
DOE
Eng
Scot
IN VELVET
FAWNS
RUT
ROE DEER
BUCK
Eng
Scot
DOE
Eng
Scot
IN VELVET
KIDS
RUT
IN VELVET
MUNTJAC
Buck
Doe
No regular seasons for rut or fawning
CHINESE WATER-DEER
Buck
Doe
FAWNS
RUT
Key:
Open season for shooting
There is no legal close season for Muntjac and Water-deer but recommend that both sexes be shot during the period November to February inclusive.
Rutting season
Antlers in velvet
Does with young

Figure 9

sex ratio has been correct, the annual cull should correspond to the calf increment for the year.

This, however, does not occur in practice, for it has been estimated that about 20 per cent of all calves born in the highlands will have died before September, with a further 11 per cent succumbing during the following winter. There will also have been casualties among the older deer, and in all age groups mortality will have been higher among male than female deer. As a result, an annual cull of about 15 to 18 per cent should be possible among a well balanced population of hill deer.

In woodland conditions, however, not only will the calf increment be higher, but natural mortality will be lower, so the cull can be increased to about 25 to 28 per cent, or even slightly higher.

In any area, however, if deer stocks have to be reduced considerably, or even eliminated from any area due to the damage being done to young plantations or crops, there is, unfortunately, no alternative but to kill any deer because, irrespective of quality or sex of individual animals, the damage will be the same. When their numbers, however, have reached an acceptable level, then future culling should be aimed at raising the quality – not quantity – of the reduced stock to the best level possible, and this can only be achieved by killing old and inferior animals, and all late calves. The most important thing to remember, however, is that once you have got your March stock and sex ratio correct, you should not ease up on the hind cull, for it is the hind that will produce the new entry, and will be responsible for a return to an unacceptable population level.

To increase the proportion of mature stags for sporting purposes, the main part of the stag cull should be taken from the younger class, concentrating on the poorer quality which will include any yearlings with spike antlers shorter than ear length. About 12½ per cent of the stag cull will probably have to be weak calves. Many stags will remain as 5- or 6-pointers all their lives and these must be shot, as well as switches and hummels etc., bearing in mind that the majority of highland stags will

5 Hummels and switches should always be shot.

6 Royals and other trophy stags should be spared until they are at least 10 years of age.

have little chance to breed before about their fifth birthday.

The hind cull offers more problems than the stag, for with the latter the presence of antlers helps with selection. Ideally, the age group from which the cull should be taken follows a somewhat similar pattern to that of the stags but with greater pressure on the older matron and any non-thriving milk hind with a poor quality calf following – the hind identifiable by its rough-looking or faded coat as opposed to the sleek appearance of the well doer.

On the question of shooting yeld hinds – i.e. a hind without a calf at foot – if they are under 7 or 8 years, I believe they should be spared, for it has been shown that yeld hinds, very few of which are barren, will generally breed earlier the following year, and early calves are generally superior to those born later. The yeld hind, however, produces the best winter venison.

When hind shooting it is advisable to take only one or two animals from any group of hinds that is known to have been covered by a trophy stag, for if more are taken you are defeating the object of having spared the best stags for breeding – i.e. killing the hind that may lay a gold medal stag! This is more applicable among woodland deer than those of a Scottish hillside, for the movements of woodland deer are more restricted, and there is less mingling of small hind groups than with hill deer which are in constant view of other parties of deer.

In any hind group the oldest animals are generally – but not invariably – at the rear, so concentrate on these animals. If, however, a number of hinds of all age groups have to be shot, the leader should first be taken and those following will probably stand about in confusion for some time, thus allowing for further animals to be shot. If the leading hind has a calf at foot, this must be shot also.

Any animal, male or female, showing ribs plainly visible, should be shot – likewise an animal with a blown-up stomach appearance since this indicates that advanced tooth wear has made it difficult for the deer to properly chew and digest its food.

Among woodland deer one seldom has the opportunity to

study any particular animal for any length of time, and if one spends too long in trying to decide whether or not an animal should be shot, the chance may be lost. Obviously, when culling the stags, the presence of antlers is of considerable assistance, for poor antlers are easily identified.

(b) *Roe deer*

As with Red deer, the ideal sex ratio of Roe should be about 1:1, but since the majority of does will breed at two years, often producing twins and occasionally triplets during their normal breeding life of up to eight or nine years and occasionally longer, a heavier cull will have to be taken to keep the population down to the desired level. From a hundred does one could expect about 70 to 90 kids to be born in May and June. Not all will survive, however, for mortality among kids is higher than with Red deer calves, and in some localities a considerable number are killed in the fields during grass cutting. Perhaps, therefore, only about 70 to 75 per cent of the kids will survive to the autumn, and this should permit a cull of about 30 to 33 per cent of the March population estimate. The number to be shot, however, could well be less than this, for allowances have to be made for deer poached or killed on the roads, which could be quite high in some areas.

With Roe bucks, well pearled antlers on broad, sloping coronets normally, but not invariably, would indicate a buck of at least four to five years of age, but any buck with the base of the coronet parallel with the ground will probably be not more than three. To a large extent, therefore, the antlers of a buck can serve as a better guide to age than in the case of the Red deer, and any buck of three years old or more with smooth antlers, fewer than 6 points or of malformed appearance should be shot. As with Red deer, about 12½ per cent of the buck cull should be from the yearling class, particularly those with very short spike heads.

Another method suggested for ageing Roe deer is known as

the Vorberg system which is based on facial coloration, but since this characteristic varies quite considerably between one Roe population and another, I don't think too much credence should be attached to it for general use. It could undoubtedly serve as a useful guide to an experienced stalker thoroughly familiar with the deer in his partciular area, but the two best methods for field work are coronet characteristics of the bucks and examination of tooth wear – the latter, unfortunately, only possible after death. Calcification of the central sutures of the skull is also an indication of age.

Every effort should be made to complete the greater part of the buck cull by early June before the undergrowth becomes too high so that you can be selective in what is shot. This leaves July and August for shooting the old trophy buck and completing the cull, for after the rut the bucks become conspicuous by their absence.

As far as the does are concerned, sadly one cannot be too selective until the cull is nearing completion, otherwise your target will never be achieved. Here again about 12½ per cent of the doe cull should be yearlings, and the remainder will have to be taken as and when the opportunity presents itself.

(c) *Other species*

Since both Sika and Fallow deer have a similar rate of reproduction and longevity to woodland Red deer, culling should follow a similar pattern. The management and harvesting of Muntjac and Chinese Water-deer, however, should be compared to Roe.

(d) *Ageing deer from dentition*

Mention has been made of ageing deer from tooth wear, and in particular on the lower grinders – the molars and premolars.

The normal dentition of all species of deer is either 32 or 34 teeth as follows:

	Incisors	Canines	Pre-molars	Molars	Total (half mouth)
Top jaw	0	0 or 1	3	3	6 or 7
Lower jaw	3	1 1	3	3	10 10

= 16 or 17

So far as deer in Britain are concerned, Red, Sika, Muntjac and Chinese Water-deer all have upper canines, these giving them a full mouth of 34 teeth. Upper canines are generally lacking in both Roe and Fallow deer, so their normal full mouth will be 32 teeth. On rare occasions, however, upper canines have been noted in both species.

Not all species of deer develop their full mouth of permanent teeth in the same length of time. Red and Sika deer for instance,

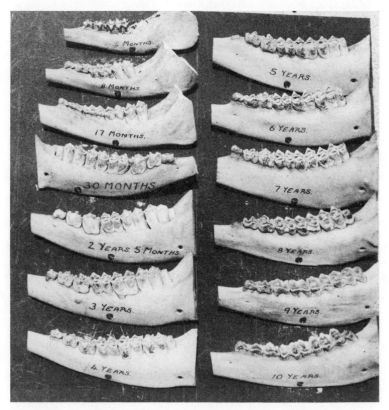

7 Dental development and wear on Red deer. (See pages 76–77.)

require about 30 months, Fallow deer about a month less, but by the time a Roe has reached its first birthday, it will have its full complement of teeth. So too will Muntjac and Chinese Water-deer.

The amount of wear on the molars cannot, however, be an entirely accurate guide as to age, for this varies between locations and type of herbage being eaten. It is, however, a very useful guide for normal field work and every stalker should carefully examine the lower jaws of *every* deer shot in order to see whether the tooth wear confirms the estimated age of the deer before being shot.

The life expectation of a Red deer is about 17 years – a Roe only about 11 – so try and build up a series of lower jaws ranging from 1 to 15 years plus for Red, and 1 to 10 years plus for Roe, and use it as a reference guide for all deer shot.

The dental development of Red and Roe deer, with a summary of expected tooth wear during its life is as follows:

(i) THE AGEING OF RED DEER BY DENTAL DEVELOPMENT AND WEAR

Months	Incisors	Canines	Premolars (PM)	Molars (M)	Remarks
1–2	―――――― i ii iii	− / c	i ii iii / i ii iii	--- / ---	All deciduous (milk) teeth
3–4	―――――― i ii iii	c / c	i ii iii / i ii iii	--- / ---	Upper canine (deciduous) erupts
5–11	―――――― i ii iii	c / c	i ii iii / i ii iii	I -- / I --	The first permanent M1 erupts about the eighth month
12–14	―――――― i ii iii	c / c	i ii iii / i ii iii	I 2 - / I 2 -	The second permanent M2 erupts
15–16	―――――― I ii iii	c / c	i ii iii / i ii iii	I 2 - / I 2 -	First incisor (deciduous) is replaced with permanent tooth
17–19	―――――― I 2 iii	C / c	i ii iii / i ii iii	I 2 - / I 2 -	Second incisor and upper canine (both deciduous) replaced with permanent teeth
20–22	―――――― I 2 3	C / c	i ii iii / i ii iii	I 2 - / I 2 -	All three deciduous incisors now replaced with permanent teeth

Months	Incisors	Canines	Pre-molars (PM)	Molars (M)	Remarks
23–26	——— / 1 2 3	C / C	i ii iii / i ii iii	1 2 – / 1 2 –	Lower deciduous canine replaced with permanent tooth
27–28	——— / 1 2 3	C / C	1 2 3 / 1 2 3	1 2 – / 1 2 –	All three deciduous PM replaced with permanent teeth
29–30	——— / 1 2 3	C / C	1 2 3 / 1 2 3	1 2 3 / 1 2 3	Third permanent M3 erupts to complete full mouth

Legend: i, ii, iii, c denotes deciduous (milk) teeth.

1, 2, 3, C denotes permanent teeth.

By the time a Red deer reaches 30 months it will have a full mouth of 34 permanent teeth.

TOOTH WEAR AS GUIDE TO AGE OF RED DEER

Years

3	Slight wear just visible on the outer edge of cusp on M1. No visible wear on sharp edge of crest.
4	Slightly more wear on outer edge of cusp on M1 and very slight wear on M2. No noticeable wear on edge of crest.
5	Somewhat similar to previous year.
6	More wear on M1 and M2, but edge of crest still sharp.
7	More wear on M1 and M2 as well as slight wear on M3. Crest of M1 starting to lose its sharp edge.
8	More wear on all molars (M and PM) particularly M1 and M2 which now have their crests worn down to give almost a flat surface.
9	Wear continues on all molars and pre-molars, and the sharp edge to crest on all teeth now largely disappeared.
10	Wear continues, and surfaces of M1 and M2 now have a slightly hollowed-out appearance.
11 and over	Wear continues, and after 14 or 15 years the surface of the grinding teeth may be down to gum level.

(ii) THE AGEING OF ROE DEER BY DENTAL DEVELOPMENT AND WEAR

Months	Incisors	Canines	Pre-molars (PM)	Molars (M)	Remarks
1–2	——— / i ii iii	– / c	i ii iii / i ii iii	— — — / — — —	All deciduous (milk) incisors, lower canine and pre-molars
3–4	——— / i ii iii	– / c	i ii iii / i ii iii	1 — — / 1 — —	The first permanent M1 erupts
5–6	——— / i ii iii	– / c	i ii iii / i ii iii	1 2 – / 1 2 –	The second permanent M2 erupts
7	——— / 1 2 3	– / C	i ii iii / i ii iii	1 2 – / 1 2 –	All three deciduous incisors and lower canines replaced with permanent teeth

8–12	$\dfrac{}{1\,2\,3}$	$\overline{}$ C	$\dfrac{1\,2\,3}{1\,2\,3}$	$\dfrac{1\,2\,3}{1\,2\,3}$	All three deciduous PM replaced with permanent teeth, and third permanent M3 erupts to complete the full mouth

Legend: i, ii, iii, c denotes deciduous (milk) teeth.
       1, 2, 3, C denotes permanent teeth

By the time the Roe reaches 12 months it should have a full set of permanent teeth.

TOOTH WEAR AS A GUIDE TO AGE OF ROE DEER

Years

1–2	Little wear on any of molars, with all crest edges sharp.
3	Slight wear on outer edge of cusp on M1. No noticeable wear on edge of crest.
4	Slightly more wear on outer edge of cusp on molars.
5	Still further wear on outer edge of cusps, and edge of crest less sharp.
6	Still further wear on both outer edge of cusp and crest.
7	More wear on both outer edge of cusp and crest, and the latter has lost its sharp edge.
8	Surface of 'grinders' generally flat throughout length.
9 and over	Wear continued, but by 11 or 12 years surface of M1 and M2 may be down to level of the gums. Few Roe, however, exceed 8 or 9 years of age.

Wear on teeth of 9–10 year old Roe comparable to wear on teeth of a 14–15 year old Red deer.

As a very *approximate* comparison, it can be said that wear on Roe teeth is about four years more rapid than on Red deer, i.e. tooth wear (molars) of a 2-year old, 4-year old and 6-year old Roe compares to similar wear on a 6-year old, 8-year old and 10-year old Red, etc.

(iii) OTHER SPECIES

Dental wear on Sika and Fallow deer can also be compared to Red deer, whilst for Muntjac and Chinese Water-deer, although little study has yet been given to these two species, both would appear to be comparable to Roe deer.

Hill and woodland stalking

(a) *Hill stalking – the stalk*

In hill stalking the first task is to find your deer, select the one to go after, and then make an approach to within about one hundred metres before taking the shot.

On page 57 I have suggested the best way of using the telescope for the initial spy of the ground. Once the deer has been located, the approach should, if possible, be made from above rather than below, for the simple fact is that the deer, normally wary creatures, expect danger to come from the valley and their gaze, in consequence, is generally directed in this direction, relying on scent to tell them of the approach of any danger from above. Another advantage of an approach from above is that during the morning, deer, which have fed into the glen during the night, start to work up the hill, and by the time the stalk is complete, may well be 300 metres (about 1,000 feet) or so nearer the skyline than when first seen. If a stalk is to be attempted from below the deer will, therefore, be moving away from you all the time, and the further they advance up the hill the better vision they will command of the ground below. On the other hand, although it may take some little time to climb the hill in order to get above them, once there, provided the wind keeps steady and you don't show yourself unnecessarily, if the deer haven't yet settled for their midday siesta, they will in all probability be moving upwards in your direction. A crawl or slide from above is also a far easier manoeuvre than a long, uphill crawl in full sight of deer.

During the stalk, unless you are conducting it yourself, you will be following the stalker. Make sure, therefore, that you do as he does, and follow his instructions. If he crawls with his belly pressed to the ground, he does so for a special reason, and nothing will annoy him more than to glance round and find his companion, if not actually walking upright, at least crawling on hands and knees so as to avoid getting his jacket wet.

When in full view of the deer, with no cover at all, advance will have to be made only when the deer have their heads down whilst feeding or, if lying down, when their attention is directed elsewhere. This operation is undoubtedly easier when all the deer are on their feet and their main reason for standing will probably be for feeding, and unless their suspicions have been aroused, there will be plenty of opportunities for advancement when all heads are down or turned away. With resting deer, however, the position is much more difficult, for if the day is calm, there will probably be sitting deer facing in almost every direction. Probably only one, or possibly two, however, will be facing directly in your direction, and if these animals are watched it will be possible, every time their heads are turned away, to make small advances. Resting deer will normally be chewing the cud, but should the jaw movement of any deer suddenly stop, you can be certain that something has happened to arouse suspicion. Under such circumstances keep *very* still. The deer may rise to its feet to have a better look, but if assured that it is a false alarm, will probably settle down again.

Sometimes a feeding deer will throw up its head and look intently in your direction. Freeze immediately, and even if some fly is tickling your nose, don't attempt to swipe it away, for a deer – never particularly good at picking out stationary objects – is only looking for some movement to confirm its suspicions. The staring match may last five, ten or even fifteen minutes, but resolve to be the winner, and when the deer does eventually put its head down again to recommence feeding, beware that it doesn't throw it up again to have another look. It is best, therefore, particularly with hinds, not to move at all until the deer has had a second look to assure itself that its suspicion was unfounded.

8 The Red deer is the largest game animal for the stalker in Britain, and close on 50,000 are probably shot each year.

9 Apart from one or two feral populations in Scotland, the majority of Fallow deer are in England and Wales.

Figure 10 When an open piece of ground has to be crossed, proceed in line – as on left – for one moving body is less likely to be spotted by the deer than two or three in extended line.

In the late afternoon, in sunny weather, it is often possible to use the sun's rays to dazzle the deer whilst an approach is being made over some open ground. On the other hand, if the sun is behind the deer, any movement on your part will be more easily detected. In the late afternoon of a sunny day remember, also, that your shadow, which will be extended over a considerable distance, may therefore be seen by deer lying in a hollow hidden to you.

During a stalk always approach every skyline with extreme caution, and never move over a ridge until you have made good the ground beyond. Failure to do so will sooner or later find you bumping into a hind or calf which, running off, will take all other deer within sight with it. If you are confronted by a small mound or peat hag, go carefully round it, rather than over its top, for there may be a deer lying behind it.

If when – supposing there are two or three of you – you are some distance from the deer, an open piece of ground has to be crossed, proceed across it in line to the deer, for 'one' moving body is less likely to be spotted than two or three walking in extended order. The man nearest to the deer – who will be the stalker – should keep his eye fixed as much as possible on them and if any beast shows the slightest sign of having detected something suspicious, immediately motion the party to a stop and 'freeze' until such time as the deer appear to be at ease again.

It will probably be scent rather than sight of the stalking party that will cause a premature end to most stalks, for the wind can play funny tricks at times in Scotland's glens and corries. Only practice and knowledge of the ground will give you skill at assessing wind direction. It is insufficient to look at the clouds and assume that the air currents at ground level will follow a similar pattern. They will probably not, and there may well be places in some of the steeper corries where the wind is turned to flow from quite the opposite direction. It is, in fact, topography that at ground level controls the direction of the air currents. A study of resting deer will probably give some indication as to the general direction of the wind, for the majority of animals will have their noses pointing towards the direction from which the wind is blowing.

On days when the wind is strong, one can often see through the telescope the way in which long grass or heather is being blown, whilst on days of little or no wind, a puff of cigarette smoke may indicate the wind direction in your immediate vicinity. In the old days a little powder shaken from a bag specially carried for this purpose was often used, whilst a plucked handful of light grass thrown in the air will also indicate any local wind tendency. Some people hold a damp finger to the wind. Whatever method is used, it must be realised that the air currents in the vicinity of the deer may not necessarily be the same, and in calm weather the nearer one approaches to them the more often will the wind direction have to be tested.

High wind and rain are unpleasant, but so long as the wind is constant and suitable for the ground, it can often improve one's chances of coming to terms with the deer. Poor visibility cuts both ways, for although it may make spying difficult, once deer have been found, it also helps to obscure your approach.

When suddenly enshrouded in mist, if it looks like being only temporary, stay where you are until it clears. If, however, after a reasonable wait it doesn't look like lifting, return to the glen as soon as possible, for it is pointless trying to stalk in mist. Even if there was a stag roaring nearby, and an approach was made by following his roars, should the shot fail to kill him on the spot, the beast, even though perhaps dead within about one hundred metres (110 yards) could very easily be lost, so it is best not to tempt providence.

If you are on your own and unfamiliar with the ground, as soon as you see the chance of mist descending, make certain of your whereabouts and if possible, select a line of retreat to the glen, such as a burn, before everything is blotted out. Failure to do this, particularly if you are on the high ground, may result in a wrong burn being followed, and eventually you may find yourself on the opposite side of the hill to your car or where the lodge is situated. For stalkers on strange ground, therefore, a small pocket compass is well worth taking out.

If you should be one who prefers to conduct his own stalking, it is unwise, whether you know the ground or not, to venture into the mountains completely on your own, for accidents can happen and it is as well to have a friend who can go back to the lodge to summon assistance. If, however, you should have to be on the hill unaccompanied – as indeed I have done on many occasions – be sure to let someone know approximately in which direction you are going, as this will save valuable time *should* a search have to be sent out.

Woodland stalking

(1) General

Undoubtedly, the best description of woodland stalking is 'still hunting' for in the majority of occasions, unless the deer has left the wood to feed out on the adjacent moorland or arable land, no actual stalking of a previously selected quarry is involved. In fact, the reverse is often the case, and the 'stalker' is waiting in ambush for an unseen deer to either pass his way or stalk up to his 'call' during the rut.

A good hill-stalker will not necessarily be successful in woodland for the latter requires a completely different temperament and whilst the former certainly requires more physical effort, to be a successful woodland stalker one must have patience, dedication and 100 per cent concentration from the moment a foot is set in the forest until emerging some two or three hours later – maybe even longer – otherwise the whole outing may be ruined by one brief lapse of attention on your part, and your only reward will be the sight and sound of a spooked buck.

Mental concentration, stretching over several hours, is far more tiring than a similar period spent climbing or crawling around a hillside. In woodland the deer mainly have to rely on their hearing and powers of scent to keep them informed of impending danger, and it is up to you to see that neither reach the deer before you yourself have had the chance to see it and make a speedy decision as to whether or not it is a buck that should be taken. On the hill, however, your selected target may well be a kilometre or more away when first spotted so not only will you have ample time in which to decide whether or not it is a shootable beast, but should the intervening ground provide reasonable cover for an approach, this will permit an hour or two of mental relaxation before the shot is taken – something which is seldom, if ever, possible in woodland.

(ii) *Time of day*

On the Scottish hillside stalking hours are generally between 0900 and 1730 hours, whereas in woodland, particularly during the spring, summer and early autumn months it is the reverse and most outings, lasting perhaps three or four hours, will be centred around dawn and dusk. Unless, therefore, one is prepared to forsake a warm bed around 3 or 4 a.m. on a summer morning, one will never make a successful Roe stalker. It is essential, therefore, for the woodland stalker to know exactly when dawn and dusk will be in his neck of the woods, and in Appendix A (page 164) will be found the comparative sunrise and sunset times for twelve areas in the British Isles.

On the tables the timings are given at weekly intervals and not by day, but as a rough guide, except in mid-winter when the daily time difference is only one minute, sunrise and sunset each day gets earlier and later respectively by approximately two minutes until midsummer (24 June) after which the reverse takes place by approximately a similar amount.

In England, Scotland and Wales it is legal to shoot deer from one hour *before* sunrise until one hour *after* sunset, and for woodland stalking, particularly after Roe deer, these early morning and evening hours are undoubtedly the best. One should, therefore, plan to be on the ground at least one hour before sunrise, and if it is an evening stalk, be prepared to remain out until dark. Cloud and overcast skies will, of course, delay the dawn and hasten the dusk.

Periods of full moon may also have to be considered for in areas where deer are subject to much disturbance they become largely nocturnal in their habits and a full moon may well delay their emergence from cover until it is no longer legal to shoot.

(iii) *Cars*

Leave the car well away from the actual stalking area, for even if the deer are not disturbed by the sound of the car, they will be alerted, particularly when the engine is shut off, for the sudden quietness will inform them that all is not well. If accompanied by a companion who will drive off after leaving the stalker, it is preferable to leave the engine running whilst the stalker alights, after which the car can then be driven off.

Needless to say, car and car-boot doors must be closed as quietly as possible, and it is important, therefore, that the catches and hinges on the door should receive constant servicing to ensure that this can be done. Needless to say, car radios should be switched off before arrival in the stalking area.

Talking should be reduced to a minimum and then only in whispers. If a dog is left in the car ensure that some of the windows are open and, if possible, select a position that will remain in the shade for an hour or two after the sun has risen.

In the evening a place in the shade is also preferable, but remember that in summer and early autumn the shade in woodland can also be a refuge for flies which will very soon find their way into the car through any open window. If possible, therefore, select a place where there is a good draught of wind, for a lowering sun will soon lengthen the shadows.

(iv) *Duration of outing*

Normally, one plans to spend three or four hours out in the morning and in the evening, so during the months of summer when the hours of darkness or sleep are probably limited to less than four, it is advisable to try and take a couple of hours complete rest during the afternoon to catch up on lost sleep.

If deer are seen to be feeding out in a field either morning or evening, or both – try to visit the area the following day, for deer will often only repeat these comings and goings for perhaps one or two days so if you delay the visit for a few days or week, something, such as the movement of livestock, muck-spreading or silage cutting etc. in the area may cause the deer to abandon the habit and move elsewhere. Try and find out, therefore, in advance, when these activities are likely to occur. Ascertain also, the times when cattle are normally brought in for milking, for once the farmer and his dog or tractor are about the deer will be alerted and start to retreat into the woods. In the spring and autumn, therefore, when dawn is around 6 a.m. this may require being on the spot before daylight so as to be in position by first light.

In woodland stalking, when you have become familiar with the ground, make a note of how long it normally takes to have a 'still-hunt' round various sections or beats, for these time checks will be invaluable when a decision has to be made on what route or beat should be taken when only a limited period of time – lasting perhaps only an hour – is available. This will avoid disturbing ground for which more time is required to do it properly without rushing, which should never be done when Roe stalking.

(v) *Preparatory work*

When passing through woodland by any path which is likely to be used on some future occasion for a stalking approach, remove any broken twigs or branches along the path, for doing so may make all the difference between success and failure.

Select as many spying points as possible, which overlook clearings, valleys or fields, so that there will be a choice to suit the prevailing wind of the day. A number of 'High-seats' should also be erected.

Make a note of where the deer are in the habit of jumping walls and fences to enter fields or gardens, for these will be good places to watch in the evening or early morning to cut off deer emerging from or entering the forest.

If deer are in the habit of feeding out in the field surrounded by a hedge which might, at some future occasion, provide suitable cover for an approach, trim out in *advance* a few convenient places through the hedge that will permit a shot to be taken. This will particularly apply to the removal of nettles and brambles in late summer, for if any 'gardening' is to be done at the time of the shot, it is virtually certain it will be detected by the deer.

In the north of England many fields are bounded by dry stone walls. Here again, select a few places along the wall that will be suitable for taking a shot should any deer subsequently be seen feeding out in the field. It is helpful, also, to place a large stone on the top of the wall, at the point selected for a possible future shot, as this will break the skyline, and help conceal your head as you peer over the wall.

(vi) *Gates and fences*
As well as car doors, gates should always be opened and shut with as little noise as possible. When a gate has to be sur-mounted, climb over it at its stronger end, which will be adjacent to the hinges, for not only will this put less strain on it, but the structure is less likely to creak under your weight. Once a stalker has become familiar with his ground, he will soon know which gates audibly object to being climbed over and which bars not to stand on!

Fences, particularly those of wire or stock netting, also creak when being climbed over. If possible, climb over near a sup-porting post to which the wires have been stapled, for this will give better support than mid-way between posts where the wires will bend and squeak under your weight.

(vii) *Still-hunting: the stalk*
The old saying 'More haste – less speed' could well be 'More haste, less success', for in 'still-hunting' one cannot go slowly enough. Even on the return journey, although you may be passing over ground previously covered, provided the wind is suitable and the ground has not been unduly disturbed, it is always wise to move as slowly as time will permit, carefully spying every likely place, for since you first passed through the area earlier in the day, deer are quite likely to have moved in.

When walking over muddy ground it is helpful to place each foot on the ground with the outer edge of the boot coming in contact first. Withdrawal, particularly on soft mud, should be in similar fashion. This will avoid the sucking 'plop' noise which will occur if the boot has been placed flat on the ground and withdrawn like a plunger pump.

When approaching a rise in the ground in order to spy over the other side, always select a tree, if possible, from behind which the first spy can be made and if the day is bright or sunny, select the shaded side. A figure suddenly appearing on a ridge or skyline is more readily detected by deer than one whose approach is from behind a tree.

If it is necessary to make frequent spys over a length of wall or hedge, or even a ridge, make a separate approach to each point from which it is desired to make a spy, rather than walk along a wall or hedge spying en route. The spy should be made from a position where there is a natural break in the outline such as a tree, large bush, etc.

If you are walking along a path or lane bounded on one or both sides by a fence beyond which there *may* be a deer out feeding in a field, walk a few yards away from rather than up against the fence, for this will avoid you being spotted by any deer feeding out in the field. Likewise you, yourself, without frequent visits to the fence to spy over it, will be unable to see any deer out in the field.

If you should have to cross a field, part of which may be under plough, or have varied cultivation to the rest, it will probably be wiser to proceed along the line of division as this will help camouflage your progress across the field. On the open hill a devious route taken along a line separating, perhaps, peat from heather, rocky shale or white grass, is also less likely to disturb distant deer than a more direct approach across any open piece of ground.

When conditions are dry and brittle under foot, I have sometimes been able to use the sound of aircraft overhead, or when roads are nearby, of passing traffic, to mask the sound of my own approach. Rain pattering on leaves is also a helpful ally to the woodland stalker.

Hearing plays an important role in successful woodland stalking, and no matter how excellent your hearing may be, over the months there is bound to be some deposit of wax and possibly other dirt in the ear accumulating from the dust and smog in which we live. So it is well worth having the ears syringed out once a year, preferably in April, before the buck season commences.

When 'still-hunting' there is a great temptation to concen-

10 The Muntjac is rapidly extending its range from Bedfordshire, where it was introduced at the beginning of the century, and has now reached the north midlands. This deer has small antlers and prominent upper canine teeth.

11 The Chinese Water-deer, also introduced to Bedfordshire at the beginning of the century, now has a feral population in adjacent counties. Neither sex ever grow antlers, but both have long upper canines, particularly the bucks.

trate your spying on areas where deer have been seen and shot in the past, ignoring the less productive areas. Deer are never entirely reliable in their movements and these other areas should also receive your equal attention although it may mean going a bit slower and prolonging the outing.

Always keep a sharp lookout for signs of deer activity, i.e. slot marks, fresh droppings, scrapes, fraying, barking, resting places or wallows, etc.

When following fresh slot marks, particularly in snow, should you come across a considerable number of droppings, this probably indicates that the deer will be couched nearby, and before doing so it generally makes a detour so as to take up a position from which it can either watch or scent its back trail. At this juncture, therefore, the terrain to the sides of the trail, particularly on the downwind side, must be carefully studied, for once couched down, deer are not easy to spot.

The most serious fraying by Roe bucks whilst establishing their territories occurs during July and early August to coincide with the rut, but this should have ceased by September. A limited amount of fraying also takes place from April onwards, not only to mark their territories but also for the removal of velvet from their antlers. Fraying damage is generally more conspicuous than serious, often occurring along the side of rides, etc. It can, however, become serious if the proportion of bucks, particularly the younger ones, is too high on the ground.

Fraying is also done by Red deer stags, particularly the older animals, during the first two months of the year prior to casting their antlers. In their case, 'tree-bashing' rather than fraying might be a more apt description, for a considerable amount of damage to both trunk and lower branches can be inflicted. The reason for this is not known, but one wonders if it is not to relieve some irritation connected with the approaching casting and renewal of antlers.

Sika and Fallow deer also fray at times but damage to crops, particularly growing corn, is probably the worst crime of the latter. All three species, particularly the females, will strip bark at times, as will also the Muntjac which has now become firmly

12 Japanese Sika deer, introduced to Britain during the last century, have considerable feral populations in England, Scotland, Northern Ireland and Eire.

13 A feature of the Sika deer – right – is the large white caudal disc which could cause confusion with the Roe – left – in winter pelage.

established in the wild in southern England and midlands since its introduction to Woburn early in the century. In fact, the late Duke of Bedford, whose father had been responsible for its introduction, once suggested to me that its alternative name of Barking deer should have been on account of the damage it could inflict on young trees and shrubs rather than because of its dog-like bark.

An examination of resting places, particularly of Roe, during the winter, will give some indication of the number of deer in the various family groups. The hair of the Roe in its winter pelage is loosely implanted, and during the early months of the year will be much in evidence in and around their resting places.

In areas frequented by Red and Sika deer, look out for their wallows, for these will be much frequented during the autumn and early winter, particularly during the rut. Near a wallow, therefore, would be a good place for an observation post or 'High-seat' not necessarily overlooking the wallow but sited so that the approach can be observed.

If the 'rings' where the rutting Roe doe taunts her amorous suitor can be located, you are almost certain, sooner or later, and at almost any time of day, to see a pair in action.

If you should see a doe looking intently in one direction away from you, it is possible that she is watching either her kid or the approach of a buck, so wait awhile until you have ascertained what has drawn her attention.

In frosty weather, and with sunshine during the day, the best time to catch deer, and in particular Sika, feeding out in the fields is from midday onwards, for deer dislike feeding on grass before the hoar frost has had a chance to melt out.

When returning to your car when the light is insufficient to shoot any more, there is no point in behaving in a furtive manner, and if there are two of you, walk and talk normally, for this will cause less disturbance to the deer, who are more familiar with the sounds and shouts of foresters and hikers, than the occasional crackle of a broken twig or touch of human scent as a stalker stealthily retreats from the wood.

(viii) *Calling deer*

During the rut, provided you are able to make an acceptable sound, the major species of deer in Britain can be called, and this particularly applies to Roe.

The rut of the Roe throughout Europe takes place between about 20 July to 20 August, reaching its peak during the first week of August, during which period, provided the weather is warm and sultry, calling will produce the best results.

Calling Roe is comparatively new in this country, but it has long been practised on the Continent with considerable success. The object of Roe calling during the rut is to imitate the peeping noise made by a doe when searching for a buck. The expert caller will probably just pluck a beech leaf from a nearby tree, and after trimming it down with his knife to the required size, place it to his lips and start to produce the required bleep and then hopefully await the arrival of the buck.

For those unable to prepare their own calls, a wide variety of artificial aids is available – some manufactured from antler, wood or plastic such as the German *Hubertus* or British made *Acme*, to the Orlovsky Universal Roe Whistle from Czechoslovakia, which consists, principally, of a 15 cm. (6 in.) rubber tube. All the above mentioned need lung power to produce the required sound, the first two by blowing and the last by sucking, the variation in sound being provided by digital pressure on the rubber tube. Another favourite call is the *Buttolo* – which operates rather like an old fashioned motor horn, the sound being made by squeezing a rubber bulb instead of lung power. Jägersport market the Richard Prior roe call.

Faulhaber make a set of calls from which one can supposedly imitate a kid squeaking for its mother, the call of a yearling doe coming into season, the slightly deeper call of an older doe in season but as yet without a mate, and the strident shriek of an alarmed deer. The Game Conservancy *Universal* Roe call, marketed by East Link Ltd., is a combined call for *Fiep* (the yearling call) and *Peu* (*Geschrei* or alarm call). Instructions are included but no guarantee of success!

The main problem in calling Roe is that one seldom, if ever, has the opportunity to hear a deer making the calls which you are attempting to reproduce, so it is all very much a hit and miss affair. Furthermore, the success or otherwise of calling depends very much on weather conditions; a still, warm day being more productive than one that is cold, wet or windy. Success one day, therefore, may not have been due to the fact that you had got the call right, but that weather conditions were ideal. It can, however, be instructive to practise calling on any buck or doe seen feeding out in a field, and note its reactions. On most occasions the doe will be found to be more responsive to the call as the buck dislikes approaching an unseen partner from across an open field, preferring to give 'her' the 'once over' before venturing out of cover.

It is hardly surprising, therefore, that opinions differ as to the manner in which the calls should be presented, or their frequency. General opinion, however, is that one should start with the kid call, the assumption being that if a doe, separated from her offspring, is off with the buck and hears the kid calling, 'maternal affection' will take over and she will rush up to investigate the cause of its distress and, hopefully, be followed by the buck. If this should fail, then calls intended to represent a doe in season should be tried, followed last of all, by the *Geschrei* or alarm call which is intended to represent the scream of a cornered yearling doe when being 'raped' by a buck – a sound which is calculated to bring all other bucks in the area to the 'rescue'. I, personally, have had little success with this call.

If you are calling from a 'High-seat', it is as well to wait about a quarter of an hour before making the first call in order to see if any deer are moving about in the area of their own free will, and this will reassure the deer that may have heard something as you climbed into the seat.

After a session of calling, before descending from the seat, have a very good look all round – including below the seat – for a buck will approach a call very silently, and will stand around for some time just in cover, watching and trying to locate where the calling has been coming from.

When calling from ground level, select a spot facing the wind where you can sit with your back against a tree, and which will give you a reasonable view of one or two small clearings. Preferably these should be surrounded by good cover of coppice, bramble or bracken etc., for an approaching buck, when accompanied by a doe, is generally reluctant to step out into the open, and movement among the bracken may well be the first indication you will have of his approach. Some bucks, however, when accompanied by a doe, may come charging out into the open, but it may well be that your calling had had no influence whatsoever on its movements, and the love chase would have come past your position in any event. Seldom, on such occasions, will the buck stand for a shot unless its pursuit of the doe can be arrested by a call or faint whistle from you.

Towards the end of July, if it appears that the rut has not yet started, don't try and force the issue by too much calling, for should a buck, unknown to you, have sneaked up and detected the source of the call, he will probably remember the lesson and not be fooled again that season anyway.

Whilst the continental Roe stalker is undoubtedly more successful in calling Roe than the average British stalker, the lack of success of the latter *may*, in the majority of cases, be due to the fact that he seldom has the opportunity to call under such ideal conditions as generally prevail on the Continent.

Nevertheless, one is left with the conclusion that the composition of the call is of less importance than the choice of site, the time at which calling is attempted, and most important of all, the weather.

When 'still-hunting' during the summer and autumn it is useful to have the 'kid-call' handy in your breast pocket, for should a buck be disturbed and run off uncertain as to the cause, it can often be stopped, or even brought back into sight, should it have disappeared into cover, with a few bleats on this call.

'Barking' at a disturbed Roe deer can also be effective at any time of the year, particularly during May and June, and I have accounted for many bucks by this method.

With both Red and Sika deer it is the voice of the male rather than the female, which the hunter normally tries to impersonate, and a favourite method of hunting the Red deer stag during the rut in eastern Europe is to roar with the aid of a Triton shell or ox horn. Stalkers in Scotland, to avoid having a long wait for a couched stag to rise, will often arouse its curiosity with a roar, sometimes with a cow's horn but more generally, vocally. A number of years ago in Austria, whilst waiting for a roaring stag to emerge from the forest to join some hinds feeding in front of the 'High-seat', my *jäger* pinched his nose to reproduce a nasal hind-like bleat which successfully enticed the stag to move into the open. Anyone who is familiar with, and can reproduce either vocally or perhaps with the aid of a child's rubber-squeaker, the triple whistle call of a Sika stag, can sometimes challenge a rutting stag to approach within shot. I have never had any success in trying to imitate the groan of a rutting Fallow, but imagine a wandering buck could be attracted by rattling two cast antlers together as is done in the States for White-tailed deer.

(ix) *Moving deer*

Although it is always preferable to control a deer population by stalking or shooting from a 'High-seat', when a large number of Roe does have to be shot, this is often impossible to achieve during the short winter days, and the only alternative method is to 'move' them to concealed rifles covering well-known deer paths.

'Moving deer' should not be confused with 'Driving deer' for the plan is not to drive the deer which often results in galloping beasts offering impossible targets to the waiting rifles – but to persuade the deer, perhaps by scent or human intrusion into their territory – to leave it, with as little panic as possible by their accustomed paths. This is achieved by four or five people – perhaps more if the area being 'moved' is large – who will walk in line, very slowly downwind, and whenever a deer is seen to move forward, they should halt for a short period in order to allow the deer to make their own way forward without being pressed, and, hopefully, to pass one of the rifles. Those moving the deer, whom I prefer to call 'movers' rather than beaters, should make as little noise as possible, with no shouting or whistling, contact with each other being maintained by tapping on trees as they proceed.

A steady dog might be useful in areas of dense undergrowth, but one that shows any tendency to chase deer should never be used. A dog, however, must always be available for following a wounded deer.

Small areas are generally more productive than large ones, for with the larger unit not only will more people be required to move the deer, but also more rifles in order to adequately cover the increased number of exit points available to the deer.

Rifles must approach their respective stands as quietly as possible with, of course, no talking. It is generally useless to post rifles with their backs to the wind for this will cause the deer to break back through the line of 'movers', the deer preferring to face the known enemy rather than the scent of a possible hostile one. Moreover, does, and in particular the dominant female, are always reluctant to leave their home territory, and will often double back, thus giving any rifle placed behind the line the chance of a shot. If sufficient rifles, therefore, are available, it is advisable to post a rifle or two behind the line to deal with these deer. Once posted, a rifle, even if he thinks, as many do, that another place would be better, must never change his position until after the drive has been completed.

Each rifle must know the approximate posting of the other rifles in the party and in particular, the *exact* location of those nearest to him. Each rifle must also know the route and direction to be taken by the 'movers' and any area in which it is forbidden to take a shot by any individual rifle must be clearly pointed out. For greater safety those moving the deer should wear a coloured jacket such as is worn by motorway maintenance workers.

On the Continent, where deer and boar drives are of regular occurrence, opposite each rifle stand or butt, red and yellow paint is daubed on trees to denote safe and unsafe areas for shooting. Furthermore, when the beaters reach a certain line during the drive, this will be proclaimed by a bugle call, and all further shooting *into* the drive is then forbidden.

Whenever a shot is taken the rifle must make a detailed note of where the beast was standing so that if the deer has run on, immediately the drive is over, a careful examination of the spot can be made to see if there are any traces of hair or blood to indicate whether or not the beast has been wounded. Should that be the case then the dog, accompanied by its owner and one rifle, should be sent to search for it.

Should, however, after following for a short distance, the scent of an obviously wounded deer be lost – as can occur over rocky terrain – or no dog is available – no subsequent drive should be allowed to take place until every effort has been made to recover the wounded deer. Without a dog, a successful 'retrieve' can often be achieved by all rifles and 'movers' walking in line so as to cover as much ground as possible in the area taken by the deer during its escape. Should there be an area of open ground beyond it would be helpful to send someone ahead to keep watch in case the wounded beast should break cover.

If one side of a wood is enclosed by a high fence or other obstacle over which a deer would not normally negotiate, but along which it might run when leaving the wood, it is useful to put, at right angles to the main fence, a short run of wire netting, say 15 to 20 metres (17 to 22 yards) in length, so that any deer running along the fence will be forced to stop momentarily, in its tracks, thus giving the rifle posted near the fence, a shot at a stationary target.

As an alternative, prior to the drive the rifle posted nearby should walk over to the fence, thus laying a foot scent on which an approaching deer might temporarily stop to sniff before proceeding, thus giving the rifle the chance of a stationary shot.

Sometimes, in order to prevent a deer taking a certain route, I have tied my labrador to a nearby tree where he will sit quite silently throughout the drive even though a deer may be standing or approach to within perhaps twenty metres of him.

14 The Roe deer has a widespread distribution in Scotland and England, and is rapidly extending its range into new areas. (Photograph R. E. Chaplin)

15 In winter pelage the Roe develops a white caudal disc, and unless the doe's anal tush can be seen, the buck, particularly after shedding its antlers, can be killed in mistake for a doe.

Figure 11 (a) Should deer have to be moved from one block of woodland into another, although it is tempting to place a rifle in order to cover open ground, deer will often cross it at speed, giving little chance of a shot.

(b) The rifle should, therefore, be placed some 80 to 100 metres back in the wood, for any deer, on regaining cover, will probably pause to look back in the direction from which it has been disturbed, thus offering a standing shot.

The sequence of drives should be so arranged that any deer escaping out of one drive can, with luck, be pushed forward into a subsequent beat. The sequence of drives, of course, will have to be arranged according to wind direction. Generally speaking, however, any deer that has broken back through the 'movers' – which they often do – will probably be lost for the day. It is useful, therefore, to post a rifle as a 'back-stop'.

Running shots, even at very close range, should not be encouraged, for quite apart from the greater chance of wounding, the sound of an abortive shot whistling past is only going to cause more panic to an already frightened animal – otherwise it would not be running. At reasonable range – say up to 30 metres – a *walking* shot can be taken by a competent rifle. As often as not, however, a walking deer can be made to stop temporarily by a low whistle or hiss.

The placing of the rifles will depend on the terrain. If the area to be driven is bounded on one or more sides by a deer fence, an obvious place to put a rifle would be within 100 metres of the fence, so as to deal with any deer working its way along the fence.

Should deer have to be moved out of one block of woodland into another across, perhaps, a wide ride or open piece of ground, it is tempting to place the rifles to cover the more open ground, but as often as not deer, on leaving cover, will run straight across any open ground and will not slow up until the next strip of cover is reached. The rifles should be placed, therefore, perhaps some 80 to 100 metres back in this strip of cover, for any deer, on reaching it, will probably pause to look back in the direction from which it has been disturbed, in order to assure itself that it is not being followed, thus offering a standing shot to the waiting rifle.

If there are only two of you, provided both know the ground intimately, deer can be moved by one to the other either by walking very slowly along adjacent rides, separated, perhaps, from each other by not more than 400 to 500 metres or by one rifle standing to watch a well used deer path whilst the other walks slowly downwind through a thicker piece of woodland to arouse by scent or sound any deer that may be harbouring there.

By late November or early December most of the older bucks will have shed their antlers and when in cover a *quick* decision has to be made as to sex, unless a clear view can be had of the doe's winter anal tush, a buck without antlers can be killed in mistake for a doe. The months of January and February are, therefore, the best for moving Roe deer for by then, not only will leaf and undergrowth be at their minimum, but the growing antlers on the bucks will give an indication of the sex, and mistakes should not be made.

For Red and Sika deer, the culling of hinds can normally be done by stalking or shooting from 'High-seats', but 'moving' Fallow deer to concealed rifles may be the only solution in well wooded areas where a large number have to be taken. Muntjac can be dealt with in similar fashion to Roe, whilst Chinese Water-deer, which prefer arable land to woodland, can either be stalked or driven to rifles stationed in hedgerows, etc.

When spotted out in a field, Chinese Water-deer have a habit, similar to the hare, of slowly sinking to the ground hoping to avoid detection by lying hidden in the grass. During a stalk, therefore, it is important that a constant watch is kept on the spot where the deer was first seen, for by the time you have got within shot, it may well be almost invisible, with only the tips of its small ears visible above the grass.

Whatever method is adopted to deal with deer in woodland or on arable land, it must always be remembered that human habitation is probably not far away, so anyone using a rifle must be familiar with everything that lies beyond each hedge or clump of trees; and *never* fire at a deer silhouetted against a skyline. Remember, also, that the path of a bullet can be considerably diverted by ricocheting off a tree bole or fallen log, thus placing a neighbour in danger.

For, as someone once remarked, 'No meat is better than no mate, for one moment's carelessness can lead to a lifetime of regret'.

Figure 12 Shots at deer on a skyline should not be taken, for unknown to the stalker there may be people, cattle or buildings in the line of fire.

(c) High-seats

Whilst 'High-seats' can play no part in stalking the Scottish Highland Red deer, they are an integral part of deer control in Britain's forests, for they are essential for the woodland stalker, not only for providing safer shooting in cover, but also for census work and selective culling.

The main advantage of shooting from a 'High-seat' is that being elevated some three metres (about 10 feet) from the ground, human scent is *generally* carried over the head of the approaching deer, and being undisturbed, the animal will probably be in view for several minutes, thus enabling the stalker not only to be selective in what he shoots, but able to wait for the ideal moment to fire and ensure a clean kill. A shot from a 'High-seat' is, also, much safer than one taken at ground level, for the spent bullet, unless, possibly, ricocheting off a rock or fallen log, will invariably finish up in the earth a few metres beyond where the deer was standing.

'High-seats', whether made of wood or metal, can be permanent, semi-permanent or temporary; they can be free-standing or supported; portable or semi-portable. Some trees – particularly yew – if conveniently placed, can often provide a suitable structure in which to incorporate a seat. In rocky terrain it is often possible to find a suitable vantage point overlooking a valley or facing another hillside on which to erect a 'blind' or 'hide', with the minimum amount of additional work required to make it 'habitable'. All that is required being the addition of a few rocks and brushwood for camouflage.

'High-seats' come in a variety of sizes and designs, ranging from a mere ladder leading to a seat or platform of wood supported between two branches, to almost a tree-house, complete with roof and sufficient floor space to accommodate one or two camp beds, thus allowing the stalkers to undertake a dusk and dawn vigil without vacating their lofty perch. It is essential, however, for the seat to be made as comfortable as possible, otherwise there will be many aches and pains during a two or three hour vigil, and too much fidgeting may well reveal your presence to an approaching deer. In this respect, therefore, there must be adequate support, not only for the feet to rest on but also a good rest for the rifle so as to ensure steady and accurate shooting. On occasions the stalking stick, secured across a corner or between two branches, can be useful for supporting the rifle, and for this purpose I always have a few lengths of binder cord in my pocket.

Semi-permanent seats may be free-standing or supported by a tree, and although a seat may at first be described as semi-, as often as not it will finish up by being permanent, its removal or demise coinciding with timber failure as *anno domini* takes over! They are particularly useful for watching an area recently planted-up where 'viewing life' will terminate or be restricted as the trees grow and foliage develops.

Temporary seats can also be either free-standing or lean-to types, but the latter are only suitable in areas where they can be secured to matured growing timber. Temporary seats should be portable. Unfortunately, they are also portable to the thief, and many a metal seat has disappeared overnight.

A portable 'High-seat' is particularly useful when the movement pattern of deer in a new area is uncertain, or a temporary seat has to be rushed into position in order to deal with some marauder. Constructed basically of an aluminium alloy so as to be both light and non-corroding, the portable seat, with a total weight of under 28 kg. (62 lb.) should be capable of being dismantled into sections so as to be easily portable through thick cover. The fact that they are metal, however, does not exclude them from regular routine inspection to detect rust around any bolts and for lubricating sliding joints. Most metal 'High-seats' have the actual seat made of wood, and from time to time this will have to be renewed, as will also any hessian, cotton or nylon guy ropes that secure the lean-to structure to a tree.

For the lone stalker a single-seater 'High-seat' is probably adequate, but in areas where guest or let-stalking are normal practice, it is essential that any 'High-seat' should be capable of accommodating both guest and stalker, so that the latter can control what is being shot by the guest. This is where seats or hides located in rocky terrain lend themselves so well, and indeed can, in many instances, provide additional 'accommodation' should another member of the party wish to come along.

In a temporary 'High-seat', which may consist of little more than a plank supported on two boughs, together with a foot rest and rifle rest, it may be prudent to secure oneself to the supporting tree with a belt which can act as a safety belt should one doze off to sleep – an event that can easily happen in midsummer if one has had a sequence of several 3.30 a.m. risings, and been seldom in bed before 2330 hours.

Watching from a 'High-seat' requires one hundred per cent concentration, for it is surprising how a deer, even when the leaves and twigs are tinder dry, can suddenly appear from nowhere, and after standing for a minute or two before the seat, will disappear just as suddenly, and with it the chance of a shot. A 'High-seat', therefore, is no place to read a book although I know this is done by one or two contributors of stalking articles to sporting journals.

'High-seats' must be located with due regard not only to the prevailing wind, but also to the position of the sun which, in the early morning or late evening, can be particularly dazzling to a sitting stalker. Generally speaking, however, its location for evening viewing is more important than in the morning, for most stalkers prefer to stalk on foot in the morning, and devote the evening to 'High-seat' work, for by doing it this way round, one can be ensconced in the 'High-seat' before the deer have moved out of cover to feed, whilst approach and entry to a seat at dawn is more than likely to disturb deer already feeding in the area.

Always approach a 'High-seat' very slowly and as quietly as possible, frequently spying in all directions to see if there is a deer about. The 'High-seat' has only been placed in that position because it is in an area likely to be frequented by deer, so there is every chance of one being around as you arrive! Should you spook it, then it will probably be a waste of time to use the 'High-seat' that evening.

Before vacating a 'High-seat' a careful search of the area should always be made in case a deer has approached unseen and is standing near.

Within a wood or plantation an obvious site for a 'High-seat' is on the edge of a main ride or fire-break, and in particular at cross-rides which may, in especially favourable locations, give a field of vision of about 270°. On the perimeter of woodland, particularly when a large acreage of arable or agricultural land can be viewed, is another excellent location, being especially useful for census work in the early morning or evening, when the deer are out feeding. Once the grass has been cut, the deer, for a period, may be reluctant to leave cover, and any muck-spreading in the spring will have a similar effect on the move-ment of deer. If you want to take out a few early season bucks in the field, therefore, it is useful to ascertain from the local farmers what their muck-spreading and grass cutting dates are likely to be, and act accordingly.

When siting a 'High-seat' attention should be paid to the background so as to avoid having a seated stalker silhouetted against a sky line. Placing a seat that can be overlooked from nearby higher ground should be avoided if possible, particu-larly if the rising ground should coincide with the deer's normal approach route to the clearing. It is also essential that one should be able to approach and climb up to a 'High-seat' with as little noise as possible, and whilst for a seat located along a main ride this can generally be achieved from one of the rides itself, taking due note of wind direction, an approach to a seat less favourably placed will have to be along a route that has been specially cleared of twigs, undergrowth and dead leaves. Seats placed on the edge of woodland overlooking arable pasture will probably be included in the latter, for an approach to these seats is best from the wood rather than from along the edge of the wood where deer, already out feeding, may be disturbed.

Twigs or branches around the seat itself should be carefully trimmed to ensure a good vision and it may also be necessary to remove some more distant undergrowth to improve the field of fire. Should this be down a main ride or fire-break it is advantageous to mark with, perhaps, a log, branch or stake, distances of 100 metres (110 yards) and 200 metres (220 yards) from the seat so as to act as a range guide once a deer has wandered out of the forest. Should any extensive clearing of scrub or undergrowth such as hazel or birch be required, it is probably wise to remove the thinnings from the immediate area.

Site clearing operations such as this may, of course, temporarily disturb the deer and should, therefore, be done a week or two before occupying the seat. On the 'High-seat' itself all branches, knots or loose pieces of bark that are likely to catch one's clothing must be carefully removed, for many a long vigil has been wasted by the approaching buck hearing the swish of cloth scraping against loose bark as the stalker carefully eases round on his seat for the shot.

In areas where there has been much harassment or disturbance from hikers, the deer – particularly the older bucks – will be reluctant to leave their day-time hide-away until almost darkness, so it is always wise to remain in the 'High-seat' until about one hour after sunset, after which it will no longer be legal to shoot a deer.

Whenever a deer has been killed, should it have been accompanied by other deer which have failed to run off at the sound of the shot, the stalker should remain seated and *silent* in his seat until any remaining deer have vacated the scene. Otherwise, should a stalker suddenly appear as though out of the sky, the local deer may associate the seat with danger, and shun the area for a while.

Whatever type of 'High-seat' you may have on your ground it must be borne in mind that you are responsible if there is an accident, for many a stalker has suffered a broken limb or received a less serious injury by a fall as a result of some timber failure. This applies as much to an authorised person using the seat as to trespassers or children playing in the area. If green timber has been used – as is frequently the case where there has been some urgency in the erection of a seat – it can be assumed that within five years, depending on the type of timber used, it will be unsafe and should be dismantled. Had the timber been pressure-creosoted or treated with a chemical preservative, it should be safe for at least ten to twelve years, and possibly longer. Nevertheless, *all* 'High-seats', whatever their structure and particularly those intended for guest stalkers whose weight and agility may be vastly different to the architect and builder of the seat, should be inspected at least once a year to ensure their soundness and any suspect parts replaced. This particularly applies to ladder rungs. Unfortunately, no matter how often a seat is inspected, vandalism can soon render a structure sound one day into a death trap the following day, so test its soundness before descending.

If you don't wish to erect your own 'High-seat' a number of commercially made metal seats and ladders are available, some of which are described as portable – others not so portable. Prices range from about £120 to around £400, dependent on whether it is of lean-to or free-standing design, and suitable for one or two occupants. These include seats designed by Andrews (Arley) of Bewdley, Worcester; Martin Engineers (Breckland) of Brandon, Suffolk; Crosby Holme (Baxter) of Carlisle, Cumbria; Slingsby Peill of Orcop, Hereford; and Ramsay of Forfar, Angus. Weighing about 18 kg. (39½ lb.) the Slingsby 'lean-to' would appear to be the lightest.

The cheapest and most portable of all seats, however, is that manufactured by Hunter Equipment, for with a price tag of around £30 and weight of just over ½ kg. (1⅛ lb.) it is small enough to carry around in a rucksack. Consisting only of a seat, its attachment to a tree or other upright support is by means of a webbing belt. Unless, however, a tree with branches conveniently placed to provide both foot and arm rests, could be found, it is hardly suitable for any lengthy watching, and it would be difficult to take a steady aim except at very close range.

The Shot and Afterwards

The shot – Reaction to the shot and wounded deer –
Finishing off a deer – Bleeding a deer – Gralloching a
deer – The training and use of dogs for tracking –
Recovering the carcase – Leaving a carcase out –
In the larder (Weighing, Skinning, Deer weights)

(a) *The shot*

When stalking stags in Scotland, it is the rule rather than the
exception that the final approach to the stag, if not actually done
at a low tummy-on-ground crawl, has to be executed on hands
and knees, and in consequence most shots are fired from the
prone position. No one should be too proud to use a rest of some
sort, and one should, therefore, always take advantage of
anything at hand from a peat hag, binocular case, or even your
companion's backside that will enable you to have a steadier aim
and kill humanely.

Overseas visitors sometimes bring with them special supports on which to rest the rifle for prone shooting. One Spanish
friend – to whom I lent my rifle – had a metal bipod, with
adjustable legs that would provide support of between 23 to 36
cm. (9 to 14 in.) off the ground for the rifle, the bipod being
clamped to the rifle by two screws which, I regret to say, did not
improve the appearance of the woodwork. It did, nevertheless,
justify its use, for all three stags shot at were killed.

The bipod support of an American visitor was made of wood,
being hinged at the top, and with two pegs at different distances
up the legs, on which to support the rifle. Of the two, the metal
one certainly seemed to produce the better results, but this may
have been due to the man behind the rifle.

Gadgets of this sort are probably unnecessary on the hill, for they not only take time in getting into position, and adjusting to the correct height, but constitute another piece of loose equipment. If one is considered essential, then it should be attached to the rifle by a hinged clamp, so that when not in use, the legs fold back along the barrel.

The rifle should *never* be placed directly on a rock or anything hard without a hand and/or something soft, such as a rifle cover, being placed in between in order to absorb the recoil shock – otherwise the bullet will pass harmlessly over the target. Another cause for high shooting is when the front assembly screw on a rifle (Mauser) pattern happens to come loose, and when the cartridge is fired there will be an upward 'flip' to the barrel. Always hold the rifle firmly downwards, i.e. don't just lay it on your hand without gripping it, for when fired the recoil will throw the barrel up and a high shot will result. I know one stalker who, whenever possible, always grasps a clump of grass or heather with the rifle in his left hand and this prevents the rifle being thrown upwards on recoil.

When firing in the prone position it may be helpful to cross the legs.

For a downhill shot a sitting position will often be found preferable to the prone position, particularly when the gradient is steep, for lying in the prone position, head downhill, may soon make the blood run to the head. When taking a sitting shot, see that the heels are firmly planted in the ground, and with the elbows resting on the knees, this is a very comfortable firing position. The sitting position can be invaluable for Roe stalking in early summer when shots have to be taken over low bushes or growing bracken. A shot from the kneeling position may also have to be taken on occasions, but it is not as steady as the former. Neither position, however, is much good for an uphill shot, where the prone position will probably be the best.

As an alternative to the sitting position, for a steep downhill shot one can adopt the supine position, which consists of lying down on the back, feet down-hill and with legs crossed, use the thighs as a rest for the rifle. If this position should ever be

16 A metal bipod for rifle support, with adjustable legs, that would provide support of between 23 to 36 cm. (9 to 14 in.) above ground level.

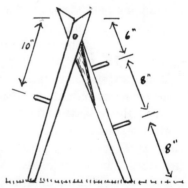

Figure 13 Folding Wooden Portable Rifle Rest.

17 Rests are rubber covered – an improvement would be rubber covering for the sides of support and also a strap or thong for carrying.

adopted, however, be sure to see – particularly when using a telescope sight – that the feet are out of line with the rifle barrel, otherwise you may end up minus a foot!

On the Scottish hills one seldom, if ever, unless attempting to finish off a wounded beast, will have to take a shot from a standing or 'free hand' position, but in woodland stalking, this type of shot, particularly in mid-summer and autumn when the undergrowth is at its height, will frequently have to be taken. A tree or stick can then be used to help hold the rifle steady, but like all hard surfaces, never place the rifle directly on a branch or in a forked stick without having something intervening. When using a stick or trunk of a tree, a side support for the rifle is probably the best, and for this reason the length of the former should be just under the equivalent of your own height so that a shot can be taken without having to stoop or bend the knees. When shooting under such conditions it is helpful, if shooting from the right shoulder, to place the end of the stick on the ground just behind the left foot, and if the calf is then pressed against the stick this will give it more rigid support for the rifle. If shooting from the left shoulder, place the stick behind the right foot. The stick must be rigid and not whippy. (See p. 117)

When a shot has to be taken over a stone wall and at right angles to it one should have the left arm fully extended with the wrist on the far side of the wall so as to allow the left elbow or upper arm rather than the wrist or forearm to rest on the wall for support. If, however, the left arm is bent with no support for the right elbow, there is a tendency, when squeezing the trigger, to pull down the rifle which will result in a high shot. Shooting from the left shoulder, the positions are reversed. If wearing a watch when shooting over a wall, it is best not to wear it on the wrist that supports the rifle, as the glass can very easily be broken or scratched against the wall.

On arable or marginal land shots occasionally have to be taken through wire stock fencing. Assuming you are within about 18 metres (20 yards) of the fence when taking the shot, if the horizontal reticle of the 'scope can be focused to coincide with the crosswire of the netting, and the vertical reticle kept clear of any vertical wires, this will ensure that the bullet will pass through the fence without coming into contact with a wire.

In most firing positions the use of the sling will be found to be invaluable to hold the rifle steady. Assuming a shot is to be taken from the right shoulder, the left arm will be placed from the outside in between the rifle and the sling, and then, with the sling running from the elbow, over the forearm to the wrist and with the left hand gripping the rifle in the normal way, the sling, provided it is the correct length, will be found to give an excellent support to both the elbow and the wrist. Positions are, of course, reversed if shooting from left shoulder. (See p. 116)

For accurate shooting it is, of course, essential that the rifle is held perfectly upright, and when using a telescope sight beware of being influenced by horizons in relation to the horizontal reticle (see fig. 17) (p. 118). When firing, gently squeeze rather than pull or jerk the trigger, and when doing so, take a deep breath and hold it until the shot is fired.

In Scotland well over 90 per cent of the deer shot at by sportsmen will be standing when first fired at – in fact any shot at a moving deer, unless wounded, should be discouraged. For a moving shot the best results will probably be obtained if taken from the shoulder without any rest. A 'scope of low power will certainly help to pick up a moving target and the shot can be taken either by *following* through with the deer visible in the 'scope, or by aiming at a spot in front of the deer and firing *as soon as* the deer's head enters the 'scope's viewing.

I have often been asked what is the best place to aim at when shooting deer. Much, of course, depends on the circumstances, for each shot will have to be taken on its merit. Firing at a target with open or iron sights, the usual point of aim is to place the bead of the foresight at 6 o'clock of the bull. When shooting at deer, the advice often given was to bring the foresight up the front leg of the deer, and when the chest was reached, that was the appropriate time to squeeze the trigger. With the telescope sight the reticle decides the point of aim, and where impact can be expected at the *zeroed* range of the rifle. All the shooter has to do, therefore, is to select a point on the beast where the result

Figure 14 Shooting from sitting position, using the sling as an additional support.

Figure 15 Supine position for downhill shots.

Figure 16 For a standing shot, the supporting stick should be of sufficient length to avoid having to stoop (left), which is never a good position for steady shooting. If the calf can be pressed against the stick, this will give more rigid support.

will be the most lethal. If the deer is lying down within, say, 45 to 70 metres (50 to 76 yards) range with the head and neck showing broadside, I would suggest a shot placed at the base of the neck, and should a miss result, there will probably be sufficient time to take a shoulder shot before the animal has had time to move off after rising. If the weather is warm, however, you may wish to wait until the deer stands up before taking the shot. In cold, wet weather, however, a long wait for a deer to rise on its own accord is not to be recommended so if, after waiting a short time, the stag appears disinclined to rise something will have to be done to force him up by arousing his curiosity. During the rut a 'roar' will probably do the trick but

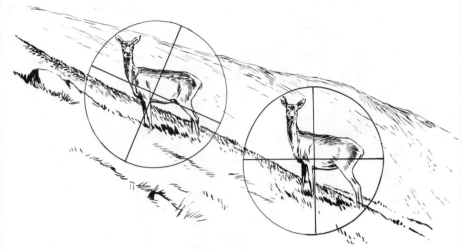

Figure 17. For accurate shooting it is essential to hold the rifle perfectly upright (as on right) and avoid being influenced by horizons in relation to the horizontal recticle of the 'scope (left).

in late August or September a faint whistle, repeated louder if no immediate notice is taken first time, may make him stand sufficiently long for a shot. A whistle is particularly useful on sheep ground where the deer are accustomed to hearing the shepherd whistling his dog, and should not, therefore, immediately rush off in panic. On occasions in windy weather, I have found it quite impossible to arouse the stag's interest by sound, and in such circumstances, a stick waved above the heather has often succeeded in getting the beast to its feet.

For a standing shot, unless close enough for a neck shot, try and wait until the animal is broadside and then take the heart shot. As with all shots, it is better to err on the high side rather than low, for if a shot intended for the heart finishes in the spine it is far better than if it had been a low one, passing through the brisket or breaking a front leg – the most dangerous shot of all for losing a wounded animal. Sometimes a high shot will just graze the spine, temporarily stunning the animal which will fall as though pole-axed. Beware of a beast falling thus, for it may well recover its senses just as quickly and be off. In such cases, close in as quickly as possible and if the beast shows the faintest sign of life, give it a second shot.

The neck shot, provided the spinal column is hit, is a very deadly one and has the virtue of not spoiling any venison as is the case with the heart shot. Neck shots should be as near the base of the neck as possible for any misplaced shot higher up the neck may only sever the windpipe. Head shots, or better still, where the head joins the cervical column, should only be taken to finish off a wounded beast for there is a great risk, in shots of this type, of the jaw being smashed, and the deer lost to suffer a slow death by starvation. A head shot may also ruin any skull required for a trophy mount.

Whenever a deer is shot through the heart, and particularly in the lower part, it frequently rushes madly forward for perhaps 60 to 70 metres (65 to 76 yards) or even further before collapsing dead. A lot will depend on whether the deer is aware of your presence, for it would appear that if it has spotted the stalker, or is any way suspicious that something unusual is around, the adrenalin gets to work so that when the shot is fired its 'engine' is already running and this results in the initial rush off. On the other hand, a deer shot whilst feeding, unsuspecting any danger, will often fall where it is standing.

In rocky ground, therefore, it is advisable to drop the deer where it stands and this can best be achieved with a neck shot. A shot high in the lung or through the liver will also cause the deer to rush off, and whilst with a lung shot it may not go further than 50–60 metres (54 to 65 yards) or so, with a liver shot it may go considerably further. Both shots will be fatal. Much, of course, depends on the weight of the bullet being used, but a Roe, hit in the lung or liver, particularly the former, with a bullet of 140 gr. or 150 gr. will generally collapse on the spot, and for this species I prefer these shots to a heart shot, for less damage will be done to the shoulder.

A gut shot – i.e. a shot through the stomach or intestines may also result in a deer being lost, but compared to a foreleg the risk should not be as great and the deer should eventually be found. Here again much will depend on the calibre of the rifle, for whereas a small calibre – i.e. .222 which is illegal in England – will probably mean a beast lost, a rifle of adequate size (say 7 mm.) will generally incapacitate the animal long enough for a second shot to be fired. When a wounded beast does get away, however, and particularly one that has been shot through the stomach, or with a broken foreleg, it is *most* important that it should not see the stalking party following up. Watch it carefully, therefore, through the glass, keeping out of sight, and when it eventually lies down leave it for at least fifteen minutes – better still, half an hour – before attempting to approach it for the finishing-off shot. This rest will cause the beast to stiffen up a bit after the injury and most probably weaken as well, through loss of blood. On the Continent, a gut-shot stag in woodland is frequently left quiet for perhaps a couple of hours or more before the deer hound is laid on. This may sound callous to those whose primary instinct is to put any wounded animal out of its misery with the minimum delay, but it must be realised that a wounded animal is very much on the alert and once disturbed again on seeing or hearing the stalkers approach, may well keep running for several miles and eventually be lost. By allowing this time lag, however, one is relying on the after-shock and loss of blood to dull the animal's senses, and thereby reduce the chance of the animal escaping. The approach to a wounded beast, however, must be made even more carefully than if an entirely fresh beast was being stalked, for the animal is now fully aware of the near proximity of its enemies. In woodland stalking, however, a shot late in the evening obviously precludes any waiting period, so the stalker has the unenviable task of having to decide whether to make an immediate follow-up with the risk of frightening the deer off the ground, or waiting until morning. Unless you are *certain*, therefore, that the bullet was placed in a lethal area, i.e. heart, then it is probably wisest to postpone the search until dawn the following day.

Deer hit in the leg recover quickly from the initial shock, and within seconds can be seen running off on three legs. Get in a second shot *as soon as possible*, and don't be too particular with

Figure 18 Point of aim for a standing broad-side target.

the point of aim, for the main task now is to stop the deer irrespective of whether any venison is being spoiled. *Only* on such an occasion is a shot into the haunch of a retreating deer justified.

Sometimes a fallen deer, although incapable of rising or running away, has to be finished off, and although some stalkers prefer to give it the *coup de grâce* with a knife jab in the heart or into a cervical joint, I would always recommend another bullet in the neck, not only because it is more humane, but also because a dying stag can be an extremely dangerous customer to tackle by hand.

On level ground, despite the advice given in some American hunting literature, a shot should never be fired at a beast standing directly end on, but if you are on higher ground looking down on the animal – or the deer is standing, face uphill across a narrow valley so that a good view of its neck can be seen

– a shot aimed at the base of the head can be very lethal. Such shots, however, should only be attempted at short range.

Chest shots at a beast standing head-on can cause a lot of trouble for unless the bullet is correctly placed at the base of the neck or *centre* of the chest, it can easily pass between a shoulder-blade and rib-cage, and if it does not finish up in the stomach or haunch, will result in a wounded deer running off with a swinging foreleg. Such shots, however tempting they may appear to be, should not be attempted, unless the range is very close. Quartering shots, however, taken at animals standing at an angle either head-on or tail-on towards the stalker, can be very lethal *provided* the stalker concentrates his aim on the target organs *within* the deer and not on the usual points of aim for a broadside shot. For a quartering shot head-on, the point of aim will probably be the leading edge of the shoulder, so the bullet will then pass through the heart/lung area before exiting behind the shoulder on the far side. Such shots, however, are for experts *only* who are thoroughly familiar with the anatomy of deer, and at close range only. For a quartering shot at a beast standing tail-on towards the stalker, the reverse applies, and for the bullet to pass through the heart/lung area initial entry may, depending on the angle the beast is standing, have to be slightly back in the rib-cage area. Such shots, however, should *only* be used in an emergency to dispose of a wounded animal. A disadvantage of a quartering shot is that the bullet, either before or after hitting the heart/lung target area, may have to pass through part of the stomach, with resulting spilling of contents, so unless it is *absolutely essential* for this type of shot to be taken it is best to be patient and hope the beast will turn more broadside. If the range is short, a shot at the neck may present itself.

The same logic applies for steep uphill and downhill shots at any animal that is standing broadside, for the point of aim *must* be at the vital organs *within* the deer. For an uphill shot, therefore, the point of aim on the shoulder of the deer must be slightly low, thus ensuring that during its passage through the carcase, the heart and/or other vital organs will be hit before the bullet exits itself high on the far side of the shoulder. For a downhill shot the reverse is the case, and the aim will be slightly high on the shoulder. This applies to many shots from a high seat, particularly at close range.

Quite frequently one can hear a bullet strike on a deer particularly when hit in the shoulder region or in the stomach. A similar sound may also be heard when a missed shot strikes a peat hag. Often when a deer is standing amongst peat hags or against a bank, a missed shot can be seen to strike the ground, thus giving some indication as to whether the shot was high or low. After an apparent miss, it is *always* a wise precaution to examine the ground where the deer has been standing when fired at, and for a short distance to follow the direction in which it went, for not infrequently tufts of hair – sometimes referred to as pins – and the odd spot of blood will reveal that the animal has, after all, been hit, and will have to be treated as a wounded beast. This is the ideal time for a tracking dog, and although many woodland stalkers now keep an animal for this purpose, it is only on rare occasions that a tracking dog is used on a Scottish deer forest.

Sometimes, also, just as you are about to take a shot, the deer will start walking away. A sharp whistle may often make a stag stop and turning broadside, may give you a brief chance of a shot. But don't waste any time in getting on him, for he will seldom, if ever, oblige twice.

If several deer are together, it may happen that after a successful shot the remainder will not immediately run away, but stand looking in the direction from where the shot has come. Don't be impatient to move, but let the deer move away of their own accord rather than stampede them into flight by the sight of you and your stalker walking in full view up to them. If the shot has missed, keep down and watch, for if the stag does not know the direction from which the shot came, it may well stop after running a short distance, and give another chance. Only take it, however, if the range is reasonable and should a further miss result, it is best to refrain from any further shooting at that animal as it will only disturb the ground.

Figure 19 Shot at resting deer. Place the shot at base of the neck near the shoulder, and not in the upper part of the neck where not only is the target area smaller, but should the head be turned at the moment of firing, a broken jaw may result.

Figure 20 From *above*, a shot at the back of the neck can be very lethal.

Figure 21 Chest shots at a beast standing head-on should not be attempted unless range is very close.

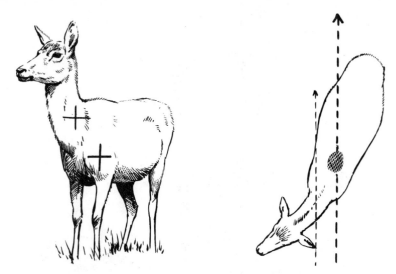

Figure 22 A quartering shot taken at a beast standing at an angle head-on can be very lethal provided the stalker concentrates his aim on the target organs *within* the deer and not on the usual point of aim for a broadside shot.

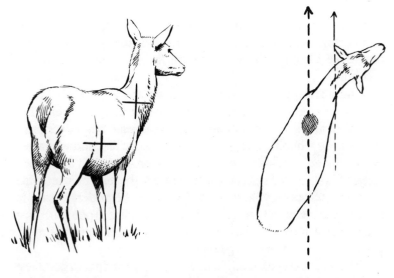

Figure 23 A quartering shot at an animal standing at an angle tail-on should *not* be attempted unless to dispose of a wounded beast. At close range a shot at the base of the neck may present itself.

Figure 24 Don't fire at a deer with others standing directly behind.

Never fire at a stag if there is another beast standing directly behind for there is always the chance that the bullet, should it not strike a bone, will pass through the first beast and hit the second.

After a shot, even if the deer is down and apparently 'dead' don't unload or put the rifle into its cover until the beast has been bled and gralloched. I once turned a 'dead' beast over prior to bleeding when it suddenly struggled to its feet and was away before I could reload, never to be seen again. It had been 'creased' – i.e. a high shot had grazed the top of the spine causing a temporary 'black-out'. A hit on the antlers is said to have the same effect, but it certainly did not happen with two stags, one a Red and the other a Sika, which I saw shot at by guests suffering from 'stag fever'.

Touching the eye to see if there is any movement is a good test to see whether the beast is really dead, or just stunned.

(b) *Reaction to the shot and wounded deer*

Whenever a shot is taken, even if the deer falls immediately to the shot, wait a few minutes to see whether or not it will recover, and at the same time memorise exactly its location, for should it suddenly rise and run off, this spot will have to be carefully examined for traces of hair (pins), bone splinters and blood – and in particular its colour – for this will give some indication as to the placement of the bullet and severity of the injury. Moreover, the immediate reaction of the deer when shot will give a lot of advance information if properly interpreted.

If the spine or neck has been shattered the animal will collapse immediately, but will be unable to regain its feet, and will require another shot to kill it.

A hit in the liver is not so easily recognisable but provided it is hit with a reasonable weight of bullet – say 100 to 150 gr. – a liver shot Roe will seldom go more than a few metres before collapsing dead, but with Red deer, the distance travelled may exceed 100 metres or more, and in such cases, before following up with a tracking dog, it is best to wait about twenty minutes. A shot through the kidneys can have a similar effect.

A lung shot is always fatal, and whilst the effect on Roe may be immediate, a Red deer may trot off, perhaps, 50 metres (55 yards) before collapsing.

A shot in the stomach or one far back in the intestines will cause the deer to hunch its back and provided the stalker remains out of sight, it will probably only wander off about 100 metres before lying down, where it can be restalked and finished off.

One of the most disturbing shots of all is to see a deer rear up when hit, for it probably indicates a shot low in the shoulder, resulting in a broken foreleg. Unless a second shot is speedily taken, the chance of re-finding the deer is pretty slim, because such injuries, like a broken jaw, leave no blood trail to follow. Any fragments of bone will probably come from an injury to the lower part of a limb, and this will, anyway, be confirmed if the deer is seen to run off with a broken leg. A shattered jaw may also leave fragments of bone.

Having noted the reaction of the deer to the shot and got some idea where injured, the next thing is to examine the spot where it was standing when hit to see if the signs of contact – blood, hair etc. – confirm your original opinion. If there is blood and it is rich red in colour, then it is almost certainly a heart shot, but if it is pink and frothy this indicates a shot in the lung. When shot in the stomach, if the stomach contents have not been spilled, the blood will be of a dark brownish purple colour. Dark red will indicate a spleen or liver injury.

An occasional spot of normal coloured blood will probably be the result of a shot in the haunch or low shoulder, but if this is mixed with a watery liquid, this indicates an injury to the chest or sternum. In all cases the deer may travel a considerable distance before stopping and will be difficult to account for.

If, after a shot, you are following a blood trail, it is helpful to place a stick or other marker on each spot of blood for this will help you regain the trail should it be temporarily lost.

If no blood is visible but only a few hairs, try and distinguish from which part of the deer they may have come, for this will indicate whether your 'near miss' was high or low. Unfortunately a bullet wound on deer, particularly Roe in summer coat, will seldom displace many hairs, so absence of these is no proof that a miss has occurred.

Never assume, even if a deer runs off apparently uninjured, that a miss has occurred for in many instances, dependent on where injured, a deer will often travel a considerable distance before there is any loss of blood. After every shot, therefore, it is essential that not only must the spot where the deer was standing be carefully examined, but also the area in the vicinity for a distance of at least 100 metres.

If, after having seen no trace of blood for some distance you should come across a patch of blood on some flattened grass, indicating that a deer had recently been sitting there, it is a sign that the deer is beginning to weaken, that the injury is probably in the liver or brisket area, and the animal has only vacated its couch on hearing or winding your approach. In such circumstances wait at least another half hour, if possible, before proceeding, and hopefully next time you come up with the deer, it will be too weak to stir. Nevertheless, shoot at the very first opportunity without a thought as to whether any venison will be wasted, for should it regain its feet, you may not have another opportunity.

(c) *Finishing off a deer*

If it is necessary to finish off a badly wounded deer with a knife rather than with another shot, this can be done either by piercing the heart with a knife as when bleeding (see page 130) or by a thrust into the first cervical joint immediately behind the atlas bone of the skull, which will sever the spinal cord. The *exact* location of this joint will vary, of course, with the size of the deer, but as a rough guide, for a Red deer stag this joint is situated approximately 9 cm. (3½ in.) from a point midway between the antlers: 7.5 cm. (3 in.) for Sika and Fallow deer and 6.4 cm. (2½ in.) for a Roe buck. When done by an expert this last named method is extremely quick and humane, but should *never* be attempted by anyone unfamiliar with the exact location of the cervical joint until considerable practice has been done on a dead carcase. Furthermore, the knife blade must have a sharp point, and if of folding design, a secure locking device.

Whatever method is used, it is essential that the stag's head should be held down and this is best done by placing a foot on one of the antlers. If a companion can help you, so much the better, but best of all, give the deer a final shot into the neck or, if the head is not required as a trophy, just under the ear. Remember, however, when taking a close-in finishing-off shot, to aim slightly *high* on the neck because the line of sight through the scope is about 3 to 5 cm. (1½ to 2 in.) *above* the bore with the result that any shot taken from only a few metres range will, accordingly, strike the target 3 to 5 cm. *below* the point of aim.

(d) *Bleeding a deer*

Some stalkers never bleed deer, believing the practice to be more traditional than essential. With the smaller species of deer – Roe, Muntjac and Chinese Water-deer – bleeding – sometimes called sticking a deer – may be unnecessary and a waste of time, for a well-placed shot in the shoulder area will probably sever one of the larger arteries and most of the blood will have been released into the chest cavity as well as through the exit hole of the bullet. Red, Fallow and Sika deer, however, should be bled immediately after death, and to do this a knife with a blade about 8 to 12 cm. (3 to 5 in.) long is required. This will be stuck into the lower part of the neck immediately above the breast bone, and with the point directed towards the heart, will be worked around until the blood starts to gush out from the jugular vein. The head and neck of the deer should be at a lower level than the body, and once the blood starts to flow, to encourage a greater flow, it is often helpful to pump the body of the deer with pressure applied behind the shoulder area.

(e) *Gralloching a deer*

After the deer has been bled it will have to be gralloched – sometimes referred to as gutting – that is the removal of the stomach and intestines. With a Roe deer this does not require much effort on the part of the stalker and can be accomplished in a matter of seconds, but with a large Red deer stag the removal of about 25 kg. (55 lb.) of stomach and visceral mass does involve a certain amount of hard pulling.

First of all, with the deer lying on its back and head pointing uphill in order to take advantage of any gravity, provided the trophy is not to be retained as full shoulder mount (see page 159), make a hole at the base of the throat sufficiently large to withdraw the gullet tube which runs alongside the windpipe. This tube will be cut as far up the throat as possible, but before being released the end nearest the brisket must be knotted in order to prevent any food matter being spilt into the deer during the removal of the stomach. In order to facilitate knotting, the flesh should first be carefully scraped off the tube, otherwise it will be almost impossible to tie a secure knot in the flesh-covered tube. Quite a number of the younger generation of stalkers, however, no longer trouble to cut and knot this tube, relying on luck to see that no stomach contents are deposited into the rib cage when the stomach is being heaved out.

In former days the testicles and penis of a stag were next removed, but nowadays there is a market to the eastern countries for these and other 'etceteras' – considered by some along with the tushes as 'the stalker's perquisite' – so now they generally remain *in situ* until the carcase reaches the larder. For Roe testicles there is no market, and these should be removed at the time of gralloching.

To remove the intestines and stomach contents, slit open the skin of the abdomen from the perineum to the brisket taking great care not to puncture the stomach wall. In this respect it is helpful, once having made the initial cut, to place the fingers, palm up, inside the cavity and with the knife cutting edge uppermost working between the fingers, and pressure from the back of the hand applied against the stomach wall, this will prevent it being penetrated by the point of the knife as it works towards the brisket. Make certain that the incision extends well into the brisket area. It is now time to withdraw the gullet tube which, as described above, has been knotted. When this is clear, first pull out the intestines and then the stomach. With a large Red deer stag the latter may take some heaving and pushing, but with perseverance it will come away cleanly. Great care, however, must be taken during the struggle not to puncture the stomach wall.

The next job is to remove the bladder, and here again great care must be taken not to spill any of the urine on to the carcase. A useful tip for removing the bladder from a Roebuck is to gently release it from its membrane lining, and after twisting the tube that connects the bladder to the penis to prevent any escape of the fluid, the bladder can be cut off at this juncture.

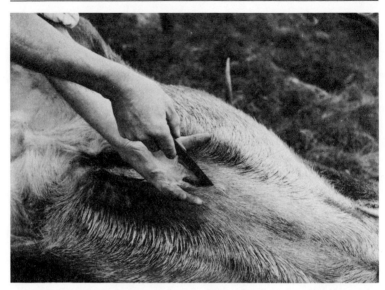

18 Gralloching. To avoid puncturing the stomach, the fingers with the palm uppermost, should be placed inside the cavity and worked along with the knife until the cut is complete.

19 To remove the lower limbs, cut the skin around each leg at the elbow joint.

Some stalkers take out the rectum or back passage after the gralloch, but the majority defer its removal until the deer is in the larder.

With Red deer the heart, liver and lungs will generally remain in the beast until the larder is reached, but for Roe, since the carcase will probably have to be carried, maybe a mile or two, on your back in a rucksack, less blood will remain in the rib cage area if these are removed at the time of gralloching and put into a polythene bag.

If the stomach wall has been penetrated by a bullet, some of the contents will have been deposited into the rib cage, and it is essential to remove as much of this as possible before the carcase is ready for conveying to the larder. A wipe over with a clump of grass, green bracken leaves, or sphagnum moss will be helpful to remove much of the mess. Flesh contaminated with stomach contents for any length of time will soon turn green, and any such areas must be cut off before the venison is disposed of.

Before putting a Roe into the rucksack lay it out, face down on the ground, so as to allow any blood still inside to drain out. If there are two of you it is even more effective if each of you takes a pair of legs and with the belly facing downwards give the carcase a thorough shaking until no blood appears. A handful of crushed bracken stuffed into the rib cage will not only help to soak up any blood but in July and August, will also keep the flies out.

The majority of stalkers leave the gralloch on the ground relying on the birds and foxes to devour it. There is no objection to doing this on the mountains of Scotland, but if a deer killed on agricultural land cannot be speedily removed to the larder or elsewhere for gralloching the gralloch should be buried and not left lying around for stray dogs to pick up and devour. Even on the hill, a gralloch left lying around can ruin a stalk on the following day, for should the gulls and crows that may collect around it be disturbed by the stalking party, their departure will not go unnoticed by the deer which were possibly being stalked. The gralloch can more easily be buried if cut open.

Having gralloched the deer and washed the blood off your

hands and arms in a nearby burn, remember to clean your knife before putting it into your pocket. Many a knife has been left by the gralloch, and whilst it will probably not be lost, it may involve a long and tedious return walk to the site of the kill. A knife, slipping out of a pocket during a long crawl, however, is a different matter and will probably be lost for ever, and for that reason it is a good idea to have a length of cord attaching the knife to a buttonhole on the jacket (page 65).

The body temperature of a deer is around 37°C (100°F) which is an ideal temperature for bacteria to breed in. In Scotland, during the autumn and winter, it probably doesn't matter very much if a deer shot in the morning is left lying on the hill for collection later in the day, but it would undoubtedly be beneficial if a stick could be inserted inside the rib cage to allow air to circulate through the body. However, sticks are not always available on a Scottish mountain, so this is seldom, if ever, done. In woodland stalking, however, particularly during the summer months after Roe, in order to promote better cooling and drainage of the blood, the carcase should be hung from a tree in the shade. If it is to remain there any length of time, make certain that the place selected will remain in the shade as the sun works round. If the back passage has been completely removed, then the carcase is best hung by the head thus allowing any surplus blood still left in the body to drain out. If hung by the hind legs the wind pipe should be removed so as to allow the blood to run out through the cavity in the chest.

For the larger species of deer, if the carcase cannot be removed immediately, it is best to leave it chest down, with the hind legs splayed out so as to allow maximum drainage from the rib cage.

If a deer cannot be located before darkness falls, provided the weather has not been too warm overnight and the carcase can be found as soon after daybreak as possible the following morning, the meat should not have been seriously affected on account of delay in removal of the gralloch. In summer, of course, when the carcase is most likely to be ruined by hot weather, the hours of darkness will not amount to more than five or six, but it is essential that the carcase should be located as soon after dawn as possible and before the sun gets up – otherwise the contents of the stomach, with the rising temperature, will start to swell and the meat will become 'soured'. Normally, however, the deer should be gralloched as soon as possible after shooting.

(f) *The training and use of dogs for tracking*

As mentioned on page 99 the woodland stalker should always have a dog available for tracking a wounded deer. Many breeds of hunting dogs are used in Europe for this purpose. These include the German Wirehaired and Shorthaired pointers, the Hungarian vizsla, weimaraner, dachshund etc., but for deer, probably the most popular are those of Bloodhound type – *Schweisshund*. The advantage of a dog the size of a dachshund, however, is that it can be taken up into the 'High-seat'. Any breed of gun dog, however, provided it is steady and has a good nose, can be trained for this work.

Whilst stalking abroad I have been accompanied by a number of these continental breeds, but in this country my only experience has been with labradors, so all reference to training in this chapter refers to this breed alone.

The advantage of the labrador is that it is a dual purpose dog that, when properly trained, can be used for both deer and game bird shooting, which is something not generally required on the Continent.

Sex and colour are probably immaterial, but I prefer a male of yellow colour – the deeper colour the better – to black, for when taken on the open hill yellow is less conspicuous than black, which is inclined to stand out like a sore thumb. Furthermore, in woodland, if the dog has to be left sitting on its own for any length of time whilst its owner goes off on a stalk, since its colour and size is comparable to that of a fox or a summer Roe, it *might* be mistaken as such by a wandering Roe.

Having selected your pup start training him with short walks in woodland and other places frequented by deer so that he can become familiar, from an early age, with all the sights, sounds and smells of deer habitat. Walks through a deer park will provide him with the sight of deer in the open and is useful training for a dog which you intend to take on the open hill. A dog steady in the presence of park deer will probably behave similarly when he first sees a herd of wild deer in Scotland. Before entering any deer park with a dog make certain that the owner doesn't object. Needless to say, the dog should always be on a lead.

Right from the first lesson, obedience is the most important part of his training, and walking to heel without being tempted to run after deer, bunnies, or flushed game birds, is essential.

During these early walks the dog must always be kept on a lead which should be not less than 2 or 3 metres (6 to 9 feet) in length, the reason being that should the dog show any tendency to run-in on the sight of fur etc. – as most young dogs will do at first – the long lead will initially permit him to start on his run-in, which would not be possible with a short lead, and thus give the handler an insight into the dog's temperament and an early opportunity to curb this habit.

During these woodland walks, which must be conducted at 'still-hunting' speed, frequent stops should be made to spy, and at each stop the dog must be made to sit. A dog that shows any tendency to whine or bark on seeing game, unless this habit can be *speedily* eliminated, will be useless for any deer work. Instructions, whenever possible, should be given by hand rather than voice.

At an early stage show the pup the carcase of any Roe shot so that he becomes familiar with the sight and scent of a dead deer. Encourage him to lick some blood off the carcase, but on no account should he be allowed to pull out the hair and pluck etc. from the carcase.

At about three or four months of age, the dog is now ready to start recovery work. At first lay a short trail of about 50 metres with either a freshly killed carcase or with a deer skin which should be concealed in some undergrowth.

Ideally, this should be dragged by someone unfamiliar to the dog so as to avoid him having to follow the foot scent of his owner, but if the dog is keen this should not matter very much. During these trials the dog should be on a long leash of about 15 metres (50 feet).

In the initial stages of training, when the dog has satisfactorily completed the trail, it should be rewarded with a biscuit or, better still, a small piece of venison.

As training progresses, the length of the trail should be increased with the route becoming more devious and terminating in thick cover. To make the trail more realistic, spots of blood can be dropped along the route. It is, therefore, useful to collect in a bottle some blood from any freshly killed deer, and this can be kept in the fridge until required for training. A little salt stirred in will help to prevent the blood coagulating. Never use the same route on successive days, for dogs have good memories, and repetition creates boredom.

After a few successful finds in close cover at distances up to about 500 metres (550 yards) the dog has now completed his apprenticeship and is ready for the real test.

For deer work the dog must associate the sound of the shot with the trail after deer, so at an early age just prior to putting him on a trail, fire a shot, preferably with a .22 rifle or small bore shotgun and not too close to begin with. If no gun shyness is apparent, on the next occasion the shot can be much nearer, and if still no sign of nerves, he will probably take little heed of a rifle shot. Whenever you do any target practice with the rifle, always have the dog with you and make him sit behind you.

During these 'trailing sessions' and subsequently, in the forest, I always work with my dog on a line length about 6 to 7 metres (about 20 feet) for I find that once a dog has been trained to work on a line, it doesn't unduly impede him, provided the man following is reasonably agile. Some stalkers keep their dogs on leash until the wounded deer has been roused and whilst still in view, release the dog in the hope that it will outrun the deer and pull it down.

On the Continent, where the ground is more open, the dog is frequently allowed to run free on a blood trail, and on finding the wounded deer, will stay with it and by barking, attract his master to the spot. Not all dogs will do this naturally, however, so it will probably have to be trained to do it. A dog allowed to run free must, however, have a bell attached to its collar so that in thick cover a check can be maintained on its whereabouts.

Never think that you can do better than the dog and start following the trail yourself for you will only foul the scent and confuse the dog. Even if the blood peters out, and you believe he is following a false line, let him have his way, for nine times out of ten he will be right. A wounded deer, reluctant to leave its home ground, will often do a complete circle before finishing not far, perhaps, from where shot.

In addition to locating wounded deer, all my labradors have been extremely useful in giving me advance notice of any deer that may be in the vicinity by stopping and sniffing the air in the direction from which the deer has been winded. When this happens, I take off the rucksack with the dog attached to it, and leave it on the track whilst I go to investigate.

On these occasions a well trained dog should remain quietly seated for perhaps an hour or more until its owner returns, and if whilst away, a shot has been fired, under no circumstances should he bark or run-in. Unless, therefore, you have complete confidence that your dog will behave in this fashion, it is as well to secure him to a tree when left on his own, for the weight of any empty Roe-sack will not keep a young dog anchored to the spot for long.

Should your dog have an identification disc attached to its collar, before being taken out 'still-hunting', this should be either removed or covered with adhesive tape or something similar, otherwise it will be jangling against the collar and disturb the deer.

Training a dog for deer is both interesting and rewarding and over the years my labradors have successfully recovered many 'lost' deer for myself and friends.

On a Scottish hillside devoid of any cover, the retreat of a wounded deer can often be kept under observation with a telescope, so a tracking dog is seldom required. On one occasion, however, my labrador did follow the track of an apparently lost stag some 400 metres (437 yards) to an ice-covered peat hole into which it had fallen, and apart from the tip of one antler, all its body was invisible under the broken ice and peaty water.

Instances like this, fortunately, don't occur very often, so a dog's uses on the hill are few and far between. A well-trained dog, however, is a good companion anywhere and it is hard on any dog that has spent the spring and summer daily with you in the forest after Roe to find itself confined to barracks during the autumn stag stalking season. If you don't want to take him on the final crawl he can always be left with the ponyman, ghillie or perhaps the Snowtrack. If you have none of these accompanying you, he can, during the final stages of the stalk, be left pegged down behind a rock or peat hag, but if you do this it is a wise precaution to leave a marker post – possibly your stick which will not be required during the final crawl – nearby to mark the spot, for when curled up asleep a dog can be very difficult to locate at times.

(g) Recovering the carcase

(i) Red deer
In former days ponies – often referred to as 'garrons' – were generally used to bring down the Red deer from the hill but today few forests have the staff to maintain them, and they are gradually being replaced by one of the many forms of mechanical vehicles now available.

At present disturbance, both visual and audible, has been generally confined to the forest on which the vehicle operates, but should the helicopter take its place, no longer will it be possible to isolate the sight and sound of a low-flying chopper to its home unit and the resulting disturbance to both deer and stalkers will have to be shared by all and sundry in the area. I appreciate that stalking is not only a sport but also, on some forests, a commercial business, and there would be no shortage of wealthy sportsmen, particularly from overseas anxious to shoot an 'instant royal' by this method, for the helicopter could be used not only for transporting sportsmen to the forest, but also for trophy selection. If the helicopter is to become part of the Scottish stalking scene – as I am sure it will – then I would like to see its legal use limited for hind shooting after 20 October, as it would then enable more beasts to be taken from areas which at present, due to the short winter days, are too remote for any serious culling. This could well be of benefit to the deer.

No matter how the carcase will eventually be conveyed from the hill to the larder, there is a good chance that initially it may have to be manually dragged to a place where it can be conveniently collected by other transport, whether it be the pony, mechanised transport or even a boat should there be a loch conveniently placed.

The rope, which should be about four to five metres (about 13 to 16 feet) in length, must not be too thin, otherwise it will chafe the shoulder or dig into the hands during the drag. When not in use the rope should be tidily coiled and hung from the belt, telescope case or placed in the game bag. There should be a loop at one end.

To attach the rope to a stag's head, pass the looped end round the coronets, and after threading the other end of the rope through the loop, pull tight. A half hitch should then be taken round the nose – or better still, round the upper jaw behind the canine tusks, or through an insertion cut through the nostril and this will prevent the rope slipping off the nose. The stag is now ready for dragging.

If two people are dragging, a second rope can be attached to the front legs at about the metacarpus (ankle), but when man-handling a carcase down a steep gradient, it is best for the second rope to be attached to the hind feet so that the speed of descent can be checked. Whenever a stag has to be man-handled, single-handed, down a steep place you must take great care to see that you aren't run down, and *never* secure the rope to your person in such a manner that you will be unable to drop it immediately you feel that the stag is about to take charge.

20 To attach a rope to a stag's head, pass the looped end round the coronets and after threading the other end through the loop and with a half hitch around the nose, pull tight.

21 If the rope is passed through an insertion in the nostrils this will prevent it slipping off the nose.

Before starting the drag, map out carefully the route to be taken, remembering that a short uphill drag may subsequently save a mile or two of dragging through unfavourable ground. Moreover, a drag over higher altitudes where the ground is often harder and the vegetation shorter, is generally much easier than one at lower levels where peat hags and bogs often predominate, so this should be borne in mind when planning the route.

If you are single-handed and faced with a long haul, if the head is not required, cut it off, as well as the fore and hind legs at the knee joints, and these, preferably, should be buried before proceeding. Then make an incision in the front part of the neck skin and pass the rope through it. If the rope can be wound round a stick, this will ease the pull on the hands.

On level ground a canvas halter, attached to the dragging rope, which can be slipped over the shoulder or round the chest, facilitates the pull and eases the strain on the arms.

On fairly level ground a stick thrust through the stag's nostrils and forefeet can be used as an alternative to the rope (see page 141) and this manner, when handled by two people, has the advantage of lifting the stag's head and antlers clear of the ground. The stick must be held close to the forefeet, otherwise it is liable to break.

On ground that yields, perhaps, only one or two deer per season, the only economical way of recovering a beast will be either by dragging to the nearest road, or cutting the carcase up, dependent on size, into halves or quarters, and carrying it out piecemeal.

When carrying the shoulders and haunches, it is, perhaps, wiser to leave the lower limbs attached, for they can provide very convenient handles with which to balance the fore or hind quarters whilst they are being supported on the shoulders, and only increase the weight by barely 1 kg. (2 lb.) per quarter. The head, if required, can be recovered later.

A long drag, particularly over stony ground, does not improve the venison, and a sledge is recommended.

There must be good liaison between the stalking party and

22 On fairly level ground a stick, thrust through the stag's nostrils and forefeet can be used as an alternative to the rope.

23 When dragging a stag out of rough ground, if the dragging rope is wrapped around the stick, it will be found that grasping the stick rather than the rope will be easier on the hands.

the ponyman or driver of the recovery vehicle, and many forests today do this with the aid of a walkie-talkie, communication between the two taking place at pre-arranged times. If two of you are working together, a 'walkie-talkie' can be useful for one, watching the stalk, to direct his companion to a deer that may be hidden from view.

For those without walkie-talkies, it is a good idea in forests where the ground is very broken and steep, to have certain fixed signalling points easily visible from various pre-arranged resting points along the glen.

In cold weather, although the venison will not come to much harm if left out overnight, it does interfere with the stalking arrangements for the following day, if men and vehicles have to be sent out to retrieve the carcase. To avoid this happening, some forest owners instruct their stalkers that no shot at an unwounded deer will be taken after about 1700 hours dependent, of course, on the distance away from the lodge or larder. Furthermore, if you, as a guest, decide to take a right and left at stags where there is no chance of retrieving more than one before nightfall, you probably won't be very popular when you return to the lodge that evening.

When back on the road and you are faced with transferring a Red deer carcase into the back of an estate car, I have found it extremely useful to have two boards, about 168 × 30 × 2 cm. (about 66 × 12 × ¾ in.) and fitted with a metal flange at one end to hook over the rear bumper. These can be used as ramps up which to pull – and later unload – the carcase into the vehicle. For a stag the head should be removed, as well as all four feet of both stag and hind. If you are loading a large stag, single-handed, a light-weight block and tackle to help winch the carcase up the ramp is invaluable.

In order to keep the back of your vehicle clean from blood and hairs, etc. Armadillo Products of Nottingham have produced a tailor-made liner which is designed to fit into most models of hatchbacks, estate pick-ups etc. Weighing about 14.5 kg. (32 lb.) it can easily be lifted in and out of the vehicle by one person, and is easy to clean.

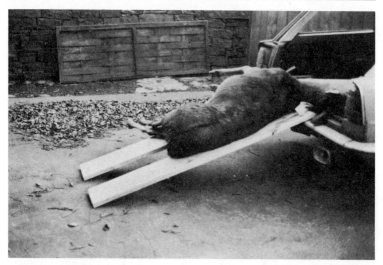

24 To facilitate transferring large carcases into the back of an estate car it is useful to have two boards about 168 cm. (about 66 inches) in length.

25 The upper ends of the boards should be fitted with a metal flange for hooking over the rear bumper.

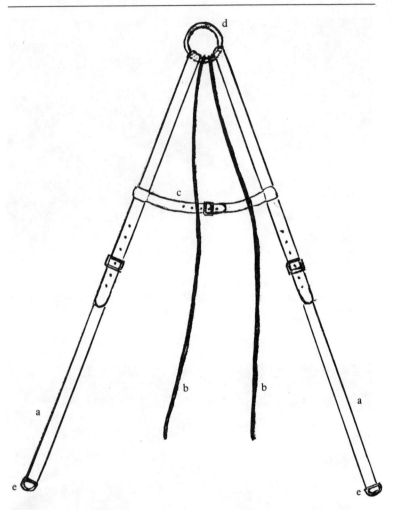

Figure 25 ROE CARRYING HARNESS.
'a' Straps 112 cm. (44 in.) long × 3.5 cm. (1⅜ in.) wide, with buckle for adjusting length.
'b' Leather thongs 76 cm. (30 in.) long × 0.7 cm. (¼ in.).
'c' Adjustable strap 1.9 cm. (¾ in.) wide to give variable width between straps 'a' and 'b' of 20 to 33 cm. (8 to 13 in.). Strap 'c' can be slid up and down main straps 'a' and 'b'.
'd' Brass ring 6.3 cm. (2½ in.) diameter.
'e' Two brass 'D' rings 3.8 cm. (1½ in.).

(ii) *Roe deer, Muntjac and Chinese Water-deer*

It is seldom that a Roe deer carcase will exceed 20 to 25 kg. (44 to 55 lb.) clean, and that of Muntjac or Chinese Water-deer about half that weight, so removal from the forest to the car or larder offers no real problem. It should always be carried and never dragged, and for this purpose one can purchase a special carrying sack which has a waterproof liner that can be detached for washing after carrying a beast. From what I have seen, none of the sacks available in this country are well designed, for the sack itself is generally too low on the shoulder for comfort, and the buckles of the straps are so badly placed as to be always in contact with the woodwork of the rifle, which doesn't improve its appearance. Studs for securing the waterproof liner continually break out. Larger size sacks are available for carrying two carcases.

An improvement is to have a narrow cross strap about 20 to 25 cm. (8 to 10 in.) long, which, when buckled up across the chest, will maintain this distance between the shoulder straps and prevent them from slipping off the shoulders when carrying a carcase.

For many years before acquiring a canvas carrying sack I used a harness which I adapted from the type used by Tyrolean *jägers* for bringing down chamois. It consists of two leather straps 3.5 cm. wide × 112 cm. long (1⅜ × 44 in.), the length being adjustable, which at one end are coupled by a 6.3 cm. (2½ in.) diameter brass ring with smaller D-shaped rings attached to the free ends. Two leather thongs, 76 cm. (30 in.) in length, are also attached to the centre ring, and these are used for securing both the deer's head and feet to the centre ring, thus preventing the head dangling down and splashing blood about the place whilst being transported. The main body of the deer is supported by the straps which are of sufficient length to go round the carcase before encircling the shoulders. Between the upper part of the main support straps there is an adjustable cross strap with loops at each end to enable it to be slid along the straps so that the width between them can be varied to suit the size of the

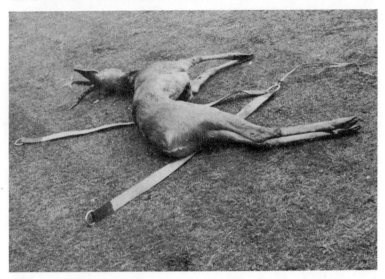

26 ROE CARRYING HARNESS (i)
First lay carcase on straps with the chest and underside facing the connecting ring for the straps.

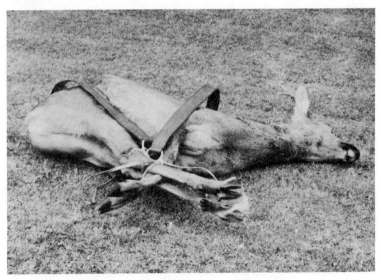

27 (ii) Wrap the carrying straps over the carcase and attach them to the connecting ring with the two leather thongs.

28 ROE CARRYING
HARNESS (iii)
With the antlers
secured to the
centre ring by one
of the leather
thongs, the carcase
is ready for carrying
rucksack fashion.

29 CARRYING A ROE
Failing either a sack
or shoulder
harness, the carcase
can be carried slung
over the shoulder,
with a hand
supporting the
head.

carcase being carried and thus prevent it slipping out of the straps.

In short, it is a 'rucksack' without the sack and when not in use can be carried in the pocket. As a protection against blood getting on one's clothing, the whole carcase can be put into a large polythene bag before it is placed in the harness, for the only parts required to extend outside the bag are the lower limbs. Failing either sack or shoulder harness, the four feet can be tied together, and the carcase slung over the shoulder, with a hand supporting the head.

On reaching the car, to prevent blood getting into the boot, etc. the carcase should be placed on a polythene sheet or, better still, placed in one of the game trays or liners specially designed for this purpose.

(iii) *Fallow and Sika deer*

Fallow and Sika deer, if shot on agricultural land or in woodland, can generally be reached with landrover or farm tractor and should not cause much difficulty. Both, with legs tied, are not too heavy to carry out slung on a pole supported on the shoulders of two men.

(iv) *Leaving a carcase out*

If a deer has to be left out overnight it might be worth tying a white rag to an antler or nearby stick to act as a scarer against any fox or bird that may tackle the carcase during your absence. In Germany the spent cartridge was often laid on the carcase as I understand the smell of burnt powder made any wandering boar keep its distance. In this country during the summer and autumn, even if a carcase has to be left for an hour or two in the day time, blowflies or bluebottles can be a problem in hot weather, and whenever possible, if the carcase can be well covered with cut bracken or similar, this will help to reduce, but not entirely eliminate, access to the carcase. Unlike most flies, bluebottles are not deterred by cool conditions, and their uncanny instinct enables them to locate a carcase in an extremely short time. Each female is said to be capable of laying up to 600 eggs and under normal conditions the eggs take about a day to hatch into larval stage from which, in about a fortnight, the adult fly will emerge.

Any carcase left out in conditions that may attract the blue-bottle should be carefully examined, and any eggs brushed off.

(h) *In the larder*

(i) *Weighing*

Once the carcase reaches the larder it should be weighed to ascertain the 'clean' weight which, on a non-run stag, represents approximately 75 per cent of the deer's live weight. Put another way, the gralloch of a non-run stag represents about 25 per cent of its live weight, but after the rut it could be reduced to under 15 per cent. With hinds, however, who have no similar loss of weight during the rut, the gralloch represents approximately 30 per cent of the live weight.

In former days the majority of deer carcases had to be skinned out, but today dealers prefer to collect them in the skin, with only the head and feet cut off, for this provides better protection for the flesh in transit.

To remove the head, cut completely round the neck at the base of the skull until attachment is only by the cervical joint. After severing the spinal cord with a knife, the head can then be twisted off.

To remove the lower limbs, cut the skin around each leg at the elbow joint, and using one arm as leverage, break the joint with the other hand. The success and ease of this operation depends very much on the cut around the limb coinciding with the joint and some practice will be required to get it right. As a last resort the limb can be cut off with a saw. Under no circumstances, however, should the tendon above the joint of the hind leg be cut because it will be required for hanging the carcase on to the hooks or gambrel.

After removing the head and feet, an incision should be made along the underside of the neck from the throat to the chest exposing the windpipe, and continued along the brisket to meet up with the stomach cavity.

The breast bone should now be cut.

If the heart, lungs and liver – generally referred to as the 'pluck' – have not already been taken out, now is the time to do it. This can be accomplished by pulling on the windpipe so that all the 'pluck' will come out in one piece attached to it.

For Red deer carcases required for export, the 'pluck' must accompany each carcase when collected by the game dealer for it may be required for veterinary examination.

The pelvic bone should now be cut so that the back passage can be removed.

Carcases weighed in this fashion are now said to be 'dealer's' weight, which will average out at about 15 to 18 per cent below the 'clean' weight. If the carcase had been fully skinned out, then the difference between 'skinned' or 'dressed' weight, and *clean* weight amounts to approximately 21 to 25 per cent.

(ii) *Skinning*

Should a Red deer carcase have to be skinned, the sooner this can be done the easier will be the task. For Roe deer, however, skinning is best delayed until just prior to butchering or putting in the deep freeze, for if hung for any length of time, particularly in the summer, with the skin off the meat becomes black and dry.

For Red deer, unless suitable lifting tackle is available, skinning will have to be done on the bench. For Roe, skinning is best done with the carcase suspended from two meat hooks – one in each hind limb – firmly attached to a beam. If suspended by rope and gambrel, unless one leg is tied to a support, the carcase will continually twist around and hamper the work.

Start by making a slit along the inner side of each leg up to the chest and groin respectively.

To remove the skin, pull with one hand whilst the other hand eases it, or by punching, separates it from the carcase. This will avoid ripping off pieces of the flesh or cutting the skin. A cloth wrapped round a limb will assist in getting a better grip.

Water should always be available for washing blood off the hands, for the appearance of the skinned carcase will be ruined if it is covered with bloody finger marks. Unless a joint is urgently required, butchering the carcase is best left until the flesh and fat have had a chance to set.

A slightly damp cloth is all that is required to clean the outside parts of the carcase, but if this is insufficient to remove blood stains etc. *within* the rib cage, this part only may be given a slight hosing down.

When skinning is complete, immediately wash down tables and floor of the larder before the blood has had a chance to dry. Always keep the door shut, and see that the window mesh is kept in good repair.

In summer and autumn, when flies are about, if a carcase has to be left in a building which is not entirely fly-proof, it should be hung, if possible, in a large loose fitting muslin bag, and provided the muslin hangs clear of the flesh, this should prevent any flies from laying their eggs on it through the mesh. If some of the cut-off pieces, such as legs, windpipe, lungs etc. are placed in an open bowl nearby, this will help divert the flies' attention from the carcase.

(iii) *Deer Weights*
Some Comparative Weights of Representative* Deer in the Larder

	Clean weight. Full carcase in skin, including 'pluck' but minus gralloch		Dealer's weight. Carcase in skin, minus head, feet, 'pluck' and gralloch		Dressed (butcher's) weight. Skinned carcase	
	Kg.	*Lb.*	*Kg.*	*Lb.*	*Kg.*	*Lb.*
Red deer stag	110.2	243	99.8	220	90.7	200
Red deer hind	58.9	130	51.2	113	45.4	100
Sika deer stag	51.2	113	43.1	95	35.4	78
Sika deer hind	29.9	66	26.3	58	23.1	51
Fallow deer buck	64.4	142	52.6	116	48.1	106
Fallow deer doe	29.0	64	22.2	49	20.2	44½
Roe deer buck	21.9	48¼	19.0	42	15.6	34½
Roe deer doe	16.3	36	14.0	31	13.2	29

Some Comparative 'Pluck' Weights* of Representative Male Deer in the Larder

	Red Deer		Fallow Deer		Sika Deer		Roe Deer	
	Kg.	Lb.	Kg.	Lb.	Kg.	Lb.	Kg.	Lb.
Heart	1.1–1.4	2½–3	0.3–0.6	¾–1¼	0.7–0.9	1½–2	0.2	½
Liver	1.8–2.3	4–5	1.7–1.9	3¾–4¼	1.4–1.6	3–3½	0.7	1½
Lungs	2.3–2.7	5–6	1.2–1.6	2¾–3½	0.8–0.9	1¾–2	0.4	1
Total Weight	5.2–6.4	11½–14	3.2–4.1	7¼–9	2.9–3.4	6¼–7½	1.3	3

In Sika deer the 'pluck' weight for hinds is approximately half the weight for stags.

After butchering, approximate haunch and shoulder weights* of adult Red and Roe deer are as follows:

	Haunch		Shoulder	
	Kg.	Lb.	Kg.	Lb.
Red deer stag (hill)	10–11	22–24	6–7.3	13–16
Red deer hind (hill)	6–7	13–15	5–6	11–13
Roe deer buck	3–3.5	6½–7¾	2–2.2	4½–4¾
Roe deer doe	2.8–3.2	6¼–7	1.9–2.2	4⅛–4¾

The saddle of a Red deer stag, depending on how cut, will weigh about 1.4 to 2.3 kilograms (3–5 lb.) whilst for a Roe buck about 340–450 gr. (¾–1 lb.).

Heavy stags. Each year a number of stags – mostly woodland – are shot in Scotland with weights in the region of 140 to 150 kg. (22 to 24 stone) clean. In 1940 a stag from Balulive (Isle of Islay) weighed 208.2 kg. (32 stone 8 lb.).

*Individual weights vary according to age and habitat, dependent on whether they have access to agricultural land, etc. i.e. Sika deer from Scotland generally weigh lighter than those from England.

The Preparation and Mounting of Trophies

*Cutting a skull for mounting on frontal bone – Boiling
and bleaching the skull – Staining white antlers –
Mounting trophies on frontal bone – Removal and care
of cape for full shoulder mount trophies – Deer tushes*

(a) *Cutting a skull for mounting* (frontal bone)

Antlers, for mounting on a shield, look best when only the
upper portion of the skull is retained. This is referred to as the
'long nose cut' and includes the amount of skull necessary for
assessing under the CIC formula. The skull should be cut
immediately after skinning, as it tends to become brittle after
boiling and bleaching.

An easy way to achieve this cut is to first cut off the premaxilla
or lower part of the upper jaw. Then place the skull, with the
nose pointing vertically uppermost on the corner of a table, and
with the antlers on each side of the corner, where they can be
held securely in place with the left hand, whilst being cut.

The cut should be made from a point immediately below the
nasal bone, through the lower part of the eye socket, to the base
of the skull.

To start the cut it is essential that a line must be made to the
lower part of the eye socket, and if the skull is held firmly in an
upright position, there should not be any difficulty in achieving
this. It is essential there should be no 'whip' in the saw, so for
the initial part of the cut a tenon saw is best. When the
supporting ridge on the saw is reached, cutting can be completed either by swivelling the skull to its side so that the tenon
saw can continue to be used, or the cut completed with a wood
saw.

One can, of course, buy a special cutting jig to hold the skull
whilst it is being cut, and if a large number of heads have to be

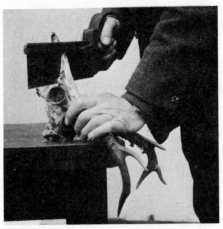

30 To cut for mounting on frontal bone, place the skull with the nose pointing vertically uppermost, on the corner of a table.

31 To bleach the skull wrap some muslin or cotton wool round skull up to the lower edge of the coronet. Avoid getting any bleach on to the antlers or coronets.

32 Whilst the antlers of the larger deer look quite satisfactory when attached flat to a shield, for Roe, due to the angle of attachment of antlers to the skull, better presentation of the trophy is effected if a triangular shaped block of wood is placed between the skull and shield –

33 – so as to present the antlers as carried in life. (See page 160.)

regularly done it is probably worth investing about £30 to purchase one.

With the larger skulls, once the top edge of the saw is below the leading edge of the nasal bone it is helpful to grasp the top of the nasal bone with the free hand, and hold it firmly until the cut is complete, for this will ensure that the cut continues in a straight line.

In order to avoid an accident, it is advisable to wear a glove on the left hand. When the cut is complete, any portion of brain left in the brain cavity can be scooped out with a knife and the skull is now ready for boiling.

(b) *Boiling and bleaching the skull*

Place in a pan of boiling water with the water level up to the base of the coronets, and boil for about three-quarters to one hour (Roe), but longer (2 to 4 hours) for the larger deer. Skulls off young animals require less boiling, for if overboiled the nasal bones become detached from the skull. If this happens, they can, in due course, be stuck back with an adhesive such as Copydex, Araldite, etc.

During the boiling it is essential that only the skull, and not the coronets or antlers, is immersed in the water. If the antlers, during boiling over a gas jet, are resting on the rim of the pan, make sure that the flame is kept low and not working up the side of the pan, and scorching or burning the antlers. To avoid supporting the antlers on the rim of the pan, they can be held in a clamp placed clear of the rim.

During boiling the level of the water in the pan must be constantly watched and maintained at a level with the base of the coronets. A small quantity of washing soda – about 5 to 6 oz. per gallon – will help with the degreasing of the skull.

After boiling, all meat must be scraped off the bone, and the small bones in the nasal cavity removed. A large pair of tweezers or long forceps will be found useful for this. Should any prove difficult to remove, a further boil for about half an hour or so may be required. Leaving the skull soaking overnight also facilitates removal of the flesh and gristle which must be completely removed, for the latter will not bleach properly and both eventually, will attract insects. If a complete skull is being preserved it is essential that all traces of brain should be removed. For larger skulls, a day or more macerating will help to soften obstinate bits of flesh etc.

Once all the flesh has been removed the skull should be lightly scrubbed with a small pan brush before bleaching.

To bleach, wrap some muslin round the complete skull or frontal bone, but not around the coronets. The muslin should be soaked with hydrogen peroxide solution, and left to stand, preferably in sunlight, for a number of hours until bleached, the length of time depending very much on the size of the skull and strength of the bleach. Beware when using hydrogen peroxide of high concentration, for if used excessively it extracts all moisture from the bone and makes it very brittle. Probably the best solution to use is a mixture of equal parts of water and hydrogen peroxide solution (30 per cent) BP 100 volume.

As an alternative to wrapping in muslin, the skull can be painted with a solution of hydrogen peroxide and placed in the sun to bleach. It will be necessary to repeat the painting about three to four times before the required whiteness is obtained. If a number of skulls are to be bleached, complete immersion in peroxide solution might be justified. At no time must the bleach be allowed to come into contact with the antlers.

If an inscription or date is required this can be written on the skull using black Indian ink, provided the skull has not been over-bleached. Over-bleaching, however, will cause the ink to run. Details on a small ivorine or plastic plaque look the best.

(c) *Staining white antlers*

Antlers which are white, or bleached, can be stained by painting with a solution of permanganate of potash. Although permanganate of potash crystals dissolved in water produce a purple solution, when painted on the antlers this turns brown. After allowing to dry, more can be added until the correct shade is obtained. The complete antler should be painted, including the tine ends, for these can subsequently be restored to whiteness by rubbing with emery paper. Antlers should never be varnished, but a good finish can be obtained by painting with a solution of 50 per cent turpentine, or turpentine solution well mixed with 50 per cent boiled linseed oil and allowed to dry.

(d) *Mounting trophies on a skull* (frontal bone)

Whilst the antlers of Red, Fallow and Sika deer mounted on frontal bone skull, look quite satisfactory when attached flat to a shield, for Roe buck, due to the angle of attachment of antlers to the skull, better presentation of the trophy is effected if a triangular-shaped block of wood is placed between the skull and shield so as to present the head as it would be carried in life. (See pages 156 and 160.)

(e) *Removal and care of cape for full shoulder mount trophies*

If the head is to be fully mounted, careful removal of the cape and antlers is most important if a first class mount is to be obtained. One of the commonest mistakes is to cut the neck too short, making it impossible for the taxidermist to produce a satisfactory life-like appearance. This is generally referred to as a 'shoulder mount'.

First make a cut down the centre line along the back of the neck from the top of the shoulder to a point midway between the ears, from where a 'Y' cut will be made to the base of each antler. Use a very sharp knife to avoid jagged edges. A Swan Morton or Stanley Scalpel knife is useful for this, particularly for Roe.

Then take a cut round the shoulders to the top of each front leg and join up across the chest between the two legs. The skin around the neck can then be taken off up to where the skull is

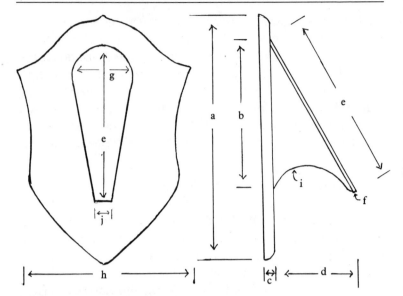

SHIELD FOR ROE BUCK ANTLERS

Shield
(a) Length 22.8 cm. (9 in.)
(c) Thickness 1.6 cm. (⅝ in.)
(h) Width 15.2 cm. (6 in.)

Supporting plate
(e) Length 15.0 cm. (6 in.)
(g) Width, head 6.0 cm. (2⅜ in.)
(j) Width, base 1.6 cm. (⅝ in.)
(f) Thickness 3 mm. (0.1 in.)

Frontal bone support
(b) Length, base 12.7 cm. (5 in.)
(d) Projection, base 7.6 cm. (3 in.)
(e) Length, supporting face 15.2 cm. (6 in.)
(i) Width 1.27 cm. (½ in.)

attached to the neck bone, at which point the head can be detached from the neck vertebrae. Try to avoid leaving any flesh on the skin, or puncturing it with the knife.

The head is now ready to despatch to the taxidermist for it is best to leave the actual skinning out of the cape from the skull to the expert, as there are several 'problem' areas around the eyes, lips and nostrils which need careful treatment. The head should be despatched *as soon as possible* after death – particularly in warm weather – for any delay may cause the hair to start

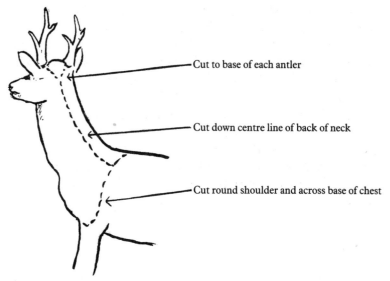

Cut to base of each antler

Cut down centre line of back of neck

Cut round shoulder and across base of chest

Figure 27 Cut for caping out a head skin.

slipping. Fine salt rubbed into the eyes, around the lips, ears and on the flesh side of the cape, will help to keep the head in good condition. If there is to be any delay in despatch, the head should be stored in a deep freezer, but before it is put in, the skin should be rolled up around the skull and placed in a thick plastic bag and sealed to avoid freezer burns.

For despatch to the taxidermist, the cape should be wrapped around the head and then parcelled up with a liberal supply of hessian sewn around it. Under no circumstances should any freshly killed trophy or skin be sent away in a plastic bag as this causes heating and decomposition.

(f) *Deer tushes*

There is a ready market for the upper canines (tushes) of Red deer – referred to on the continent as *grandelns* – those of an old stag, dependent on quality, fetching more than double the price of hind tushes. Top quality tushes, which are used for brooches, cuff links, dress studs, etc. should be large, brown and free from any decaying cavities.

The tushes can be extracted either with a pair of pliers, taking care not to damage the surface of the teeth, or with a knife. The tushes should then be boiled for about ten minutes to remove the flesh.

Since the war the tushes have generally been considered by the stalkers as one of their perqs. It should be appreciated, however, that *grandelns* are almost as interesting to many sportsmen from Austria and Germany as are the antlers, and they should, therefore, always be allowed to keep them if desired.

Appendices

A. Sunrise and sunset times in the British Isles
   (a) England and Wales
   (b) Scotland
B. Deer Legislation
   (a) Close season dates for deer in Great Britain and Ireland
   (b) Firearm certificates
   (c) Licence to kill game
   (d) Game dealer's licences and Venison dealer's licences
   (e) Firearms and ammunition
   (i) England and Wales
   (ii) Scotland
   (iii) Northern Ireland
   (iv) Eire
C.
   (a) Medal categories for British Deer (native and exotic)
   (b) Britain's best recorded medal trophies
   (c) What to look for in a trophy head.

Appendix A
Sun Risings and Settings

Legend		*Lat.*	*Long.*
Column 1 based on Greenwich Mean time (south-east)		51.28 N	0.00
Column 2 based on Bristol (south-west)		51.27 N	2.35 W
Column 3 based on Cannock (mid-England)		52.42 N	2.01 W
Column 4 based on Newcastle on Tyne (north-east)		54.59 N	1.35 W
Column 5 based on Kendal (north-west)		54.20 N	2.45 W
Column 6 based on Rhayadar (mid-Wales)		52.18 N	3.30 W

(i) ENGLAND AND WALES

		1 SOUTH-EAST		2 SOUTH-WEST		3 MID-ENGLAND		4 NORTH-EAST		5 NORTH-WEST		6 MID-WALES	
		Rises	Sets	Rises	Sets	Rises	Sets	Rises	Sets	Rises	Sets	Rises	Sets
Jan.	1	0806	1601	0816	1612	0819	1605	0831	1548	0833	1558	0824	1612
	8	0805	1609	0815	1620	0817	1612	0829	1557	0829	1606	0822	1619
	15	0800	1619	0810	1630	0814	1621	0823	1609	0825	1616	0818	1628
	22	0753	1631	0803	1641	0804	1636	0815	1621	0815	1633	0805	1643
	29	0744	1643	0754	1653	0756	1647	0804	1636	0806	1644	0801	1655
Feb.	5	0734	1656	0743	1706	0746	1658	0751	1650	0754	1656	0751	1706
	12	0722	1708	0732	1718	0730	1715	0737	1705	0737	1712	0735	1723
	19	0708	1721	0718	1731	0718	1726	0721	1720	0724	1727	0727	1730
	26	0653	1734	0703	1744	0705	1738	0705	1734	0710	1739	0713	1746
Mar.	5	0639	1745	0648	1755	0645	1755	0648	1748	0649	1755	0650	1802
	12	0623	1758	0633	1808	0631	1806	0631	1803	0634	1810	0636	1813
	19	0607	1810	0617	1820	0617	1817	0613	1816	0619	1820	0622	1823
(a)						start of summer time							
	20	0705	1912	0715	1922	0715	1920	0711	1918	0716	1922	0720	1926
	26	0651	1922	0701	1932	0658	1931	0656	1929	0657	1937	0701	1939
Apr.	2	0636	1934	0646	1943	0641	1943	0638	1943	0642	1948	0648	1949
	9	0620	1945	0630	1955	0625	1956	0620	1957	0628	1959	0634	1959
	16	0604	1957	0614	2007	0606	2009	0603	2010	0606	2017	0613	2015
	23	0549	2009	0559	2019	0554	2020	0546	2024	0552	2028	0600	2026
	30	0536	2021	0546	2030	0538	2031	0530	2037	0539	2041	0548	2036
May	7	0523	2031	0533	2041	0526	2042	0515	2051	0520	2056	0531	2051
	14	0511	2042	0521	2052	0515	2055	0502	2104	0510	2106	0521	2101
	21	0501	2053	0511	2103	0504	2106	0450	2116	0459	2117	0511	2110
	28	0453	2102	0503	2112	0455	2116	0440	2127	0447	2130	0501	2122
June	4	0447	2110	0457	2119	0449	2124	0433	2136	0441	2138	0456	2125
	11	0443	2116	0453	2126	0446	2129	0427	2143	0438	2143	0453	2130
	18	0442	2120	0452	2130	0444	2134	0426	2148	0435	2150	0451	2139
(c)	25	0443	2121	0453	2131	0445	2135	0427	2149	0436	2149	0453	2140
July	2	0447	2120	0457	2130	0449	2134	0431	2148	0440	2149	0456	2139
	9	0453	2117	0503	2126	0456	2129	0438	2143	0448	2144	0504	2134
	16	0500	2111	0511	2121	0503	2124	0447	2136	0457	2136	0512	2129
	23	0509	2103	0520	2113	0516	2118	0458	2126	0505	2128	0518	2122
	30	0519	2053	0529	2103	0520	2105	0509	2114	0520	2114	0531	2109

		1 SOUTH-EAST		2 SOUTH-WEST		3 MID-ENGLAND		4 NORTH-EAST		5 NORTH-WEST		6 MID-WALES	
		Rises	Sets	Rises	Sets	Rises	Sets	Rises	Sets	Rises	Sets	Rises	Sets
Aug.	6	0530	2041	0540	2051	0534	2053	0522	2100	0531	2102	0541	2058
	13	0541	2029	0551	2038	0545	2042	0535	2046	0544	2049	0550	2046
	20	0552	2014	0602	2024	0559	2023	0548	2030	0558	2029	0606	2027
	27	0603	1959	0613	2009	0610	2009	0601	2013	0609	2015	0616	2014
Sep.	3	0614	1944	0624	1954	0620	1955	0614	1956	0620	1950	0626	2000
	10	0626	1928	0636	1937	0635	1934	0627	1938	0636	1938	0641	1939
	17	0636	1912	0646	1922	0645	1919	0641	1920	0647	1923	0651	1925
	24	0648	1856	0658	1906	0655	1905	0653	1902	0658	1908	0701	1911
Oct.	1	0659	1840	0709	1850	0710	1844	0706	1845	0714	1846	0716	1850
	8	0711	1824	0720	1834	0720	1829	0720	1826	0725	1831	0726	1836
	15	0722	1809	0732	1819	0732	1816	0733	1810	0736	1817	0736	1823
	22	0734	1754	0744	1804	0748	1756	0747	1753	0754	1756	0752	1804
(b)						End of summer time							
	29	0647	1640	0657	1650	0659	1644	0702	1637	0706	1643	0703	1652
Nov.	5	0659	1628	0709	1638	0710	1632	0716	1623	0718	1631	0709	1646
	12	0711	1616	0721	1626	0727	1616	0730	1609	0736	1614	0731	1625
	19	0723	1607	0733	1617	0738	1608	0744	1558	0748	1605	0741	1617
	26	0735	1559	0745	1609	0748	1601	0757	1549	0758	1556	0751	1610
Dec.	3	0745	1554	0755	1605	0801	1554	0809	1542	0813	1549	0805	1603
	10	0754	1551	0804	1602	0808	1552	0819	1538	0820	1547	0812	1601
	17	0801	1552	0810	1602	0812	1552	0826	1538	0826	1547	0818	1600
(d)	24	0805	1555	0814	1605	0820	1555	0830	1541	0832	1550	0823	1605
	31	0807	1600	0816	1611	0821	1600	0832	1546	0832	1556	0824	1610

Sun Risings and Settings

Legend

		Lat.	Long.
Column 7	Based on Selkirk (south-east)	55.33 N	2.50 W
Column 8	Based on Newton Stewart (south-west)	54.57 N	4.29 W
Column 9	Based on Glasgow (mid-Scotland)	55.53 N	4.15 W
Column 10	Based on Aberdeen (north-east)	57.10 N	2.04 W
Column 11	Based on Ullapool (north-west)	57.54 N	5.10 W
Column 12	Based on Tongue (far north)	58.29 N	4.25 W

(ii) SCOTLAND

		7 SOUTH-EAST		8 SOUTH-WEST		9 MID-SCOTLAND		10 NORTH-EAST		11 NORTH-WEST		12 FAR NORTH	
		Rises	Sets	Rises	Sets	Rises	Sets	Rises	Sets	Rises	Sets	Rises	Sets
Jan.	1	0839	1551	0843	1601	0848	1554	0847	1539	0906	1544	0907	1536
	8	0836	1600	0840	1608	0845	1603	0843	1548	0902	1553	0903	1546
	15	0831	1610	0835	1619	0839	1615	0838	1558	0856	1604	0857	1558
	22	0820	1626	0825	1636	0830	1626	0826	1615	0843	1624	0843	1618
	29	0810	1639	0815	1648	0818	1643	0815	1628	0832	1637	0832	1632
Feb.	5	0759	1652	0804	1702	0805	1658	0803	1644	0819	1652	0819	1646
	12	0741	1711	0746	1719	0751	1713	0742	1704	0758	1711	0800	1708
	19	0727	1724	0733	1732	0735	1728	0728	1718	0743	1728	0742	1725
	26	0712	1737	0718	1745	0718	1743	0713	1731	0728	1742	0726	1737
Mar.	5	0651	1755	0657	1803	0701	1758	0649	1751	0705	1803	0701	1759
	12	0635	1808	0641	1816	0643	1813	0633	1804	0647	1816	0644	1812
	19	0620	1820	0626	1827	0624	1827	0617	1817	0630	1830	0624	1829

		7 SOUTH-EAST		8 SOUTH-WEST		9 MID-SCOTLAND		10 NORTH-EAST		11 NORTH-WEST		12 FAR NORTH	
		Rises	Sets	Rises	Sets	Rises	Sets	Rises	Sets	Rises	Sets	Rises	Sets
(a)						Start of summer time							
	20	0712	1926	0724	1930	0722	1929	0715	1920	0728	1933	0720	1932
	26	0656	1938	0704	1944	0706	1941	0652	1936	0704	1950	0701	1947
Apr.	2	0640	1951	0648	1957	0647	1956	0635	1949	0647	2003	0644	2001
	9	0625	2002	0633	2008	0629	2010	0617	2004	0631	2017	0627	2015
	16	0603	2020	0611	2025	0611	2024	0554	2022	0610	2035	0600	2035
	23	0548	2032	0557	2037	0554	2038	0540	2034	0552	2050	0545	2049
	30	0534	2044	0543	2049	0538	2051	0525	2048	0535	2104	0530	2103
May	7	0515	2102	0524	2107	0523	2105	0504	2107	0516	2122	0505	2124
	14	0503	2113	0513	2117	0509	2119	0452	2118	0500	2134	0454	2136
	21	0453	2128	0502	2127	0456	2132	0440	2131	0448	2149	0441	2150
	28	0440	2138	0450	2142	0446	2143	0426	2146	0433	2205	0426	2206
June	4	0433	2146	0445	2149	0438	2153	0422	2151	0425	2214	0418	2216
	11	0429	2152	0440	2155	0432	2200	0411	2202	0420	2221	0414	2223
	18	0427	2158	0438	2201	0430	2205	0410	2208	0417	2228	0412	2230
(c)	25	0428	2159	0439	2201	0432	2207	0412	2209	0418	2228	0420	2229
July	2	0433	2157	0444	2200	0436	2205	0416	2207	0423	2226	0415	2228
	9	0441	2150	0451	2153	0443	2200	0426	2159	0433	2218	0426	2219
	16	0450	2143	0500	2147	0453	2152	0435	2153	0442	2210	0435	2211
	23	0459	2134	0508	2138	0504	2142	0445	2142	0453	2200	0446	2201
	30	0514	2119	0524	2123	0516	2129	0504	2124	0511	2145	0505	2145
Aug.	6	0525	2107	0535	2112	0529	2115	0515	2104	0524	2129	0518	2129
	13	0537	2054	0546	2059	0543	2100	0527	2050	0537	2114	0532	2114
	20	0555	2032	0603	2038	0556	2044	0546	2035	0552	2055	0550	2052
	27	0605	2018	0614	2024	0609	2027	0559	2019	0609	2035	0604	2035
Sep.	3	0617	2003	0625	2009	0623	2009	0611	2003	0622	2018	0618	2016
	10	0634	1940	0642	1946	0637	1950	0629	1939	0639	1955	0637	1951
	17	0646	1924	0654	1930	0651	1932	0642	1922	0654	1936	0651	1933
	24	0657	1908	0705	1915	0704	1913	0654	1906	0707	1919	0704	1916
Oct.	1	0715	1845	0721	1853	0718	1855	0713	1842	0725	1856	0723	1850
	8	0727	1829	0733	1837	0732	1836	0726	1825	0740	1837	0737	1833
	15	0739	1814	0745	1822	0746	1819	0738	1809	0753	1820	0751	1816
	22	0757	1753	0802	1801	0801	1801	0758	1747	1812	1800	0811	1752
(b)						Summer time ends							
	29	0710	1639	0715	1648	0716	1645	0712	1631	0727	1641	0726	1636
Nov.	5	0722	1627	0728	1636	0730	1631	0725	1617	0741	1627	0740	1622
	12	0741	1609	0746	1618	0744	1617	0743	1600	0802	1608	0802	1602
	19	0753	1559	0758	1609	0759	1605	0758	1548	0816	1556	0816	1549
	26	0805	1551	0808	1601	0812	1555	0810	1539	0828	1547	0829	1540
Dec.	3	0820	1542	0823	1553	0825	1548	0827	1529	0845	1536	0846	1529
	10	0827	1539	0831	1550	0835	1544	0836	1526	0855	1533	0856	1526
	17	0834	1539	0837	1549	0842	1543	0843	1526	0902	1531	0903	1524
(d)	24	0839	1543	0843	1553	0847	1546	0848	1528	0907	1535	0908	1528
	31	0840	1548	0844	1558	0848	1552	0849	1533	0907	1541	0908	1532

NOTE (a) Summer time commences late March, so clock times, thereafter, will be one hour LATER.

(b) Summer time ends late October, so clock times, thereafter, will be one hour EARLIER.

(c) After 22 June (longest day), sunrise starts to get later each day.

(d) After 22 December (shortest day), sunrise starts to get earlier each day.

(e) The timings given are reasonably accurate for the area in question, but for any intermediate locality can be increased or reduced accordingly, i.e. at Greenwich on 7 May sunrise is at 0523, whilst at Bristol – some 120 miles to the west – it is at 0533. In the Swindon/Marlborough area, therefore, which is about midway, sunrise will be about 0528 on 7 May.

Appendix B
Deer Legislation

(a) *Close Season Dates for Deer in Great Britain and Ireland. All dates inclusive*

	Scotland (1)	England & Wales (2)	Northern Ireland (4)	Eire (5)
RED DEER				
stags	21 Oct.–30 June	1 May–31 July	1 May–31 July	1 March–31 Aug.*
hinds	16 Feb.–20 Oct.	1 March–31 Oct.	1 March–31 Oct.	1 March–31 Oct.*
SIKA DEER				
stags	21 Oct.–30 June (3)	1 May–31 July	1 May–31 July	1 March–31 Aug.
hinds	16 Feb.–20 Oct.	1 March–31 Oct.	1 March–31 Oct.	1 March–31 Oct.
RED/SIKA HYBRID				
stags	21 Oct.–30 June (3)	1 May–31 July	1 May–31 July	1 March–31 Aug.
hinds	16 Feb.–20 Oct.	1 March–31 Oct.	1 March–31 Oct.	1 March–31 Oct.
FALLOW DEER				
bucks	1 May–31 July (3)	1 May–31 July	1 May–31 July	1 March–31 Aug.
does	16 Feb.–20 Oct.	1 March–31 Oct.	1 March–31 Oct.	1 March–31 Oct.
ROE DEER				
bucks	21 Oct.–31 March (3)	1 Nov.–31 March	*No open season for Red deer in Co.	
does	1 Apr.–20 Oct. (3)	1 March–31 Oct.	Kerry.	
MUNTJAC				
bucks } does }	No legal close season. Recommended both sexes should have have close season 1 March–31 Oct.			
CHINESE WATER-DEER				
bucks } does }	No legal close season. Recommended both sexes should have close season 1 March–31 Oct.			

1. Under the *Deer (Scotland) Act* 1959
2. Under the *Deer Act* 1991
3. Under the *Deer (Close Seasons) (Scotland) Order* 1984
4. Under the *Wildlife (Northern Ireland) Order* 1985
5. Under the *Wildlife (Wild Mammals) (Open Seasons) Order* 1979

Note: A deer may only be killed during the close season by the occupier of the land or an *authorised* person if it can be shown that serious damage was, or would be, caused to crops, growing timber etc. Details of the exceptions must be obtained from the relevant Act or Order.

(b) *Firearm Certificate*

No one in Britain is permitted to own or use a rifle unless in possession of a Firearm Certificate obtained from the police at a cost of £46, and valid for three years. Before issuing a certificate, the police will require to know where the rifle is to be used, and unless they are prepared to issue an 'open' licence, will enter the area on the certificate where the rifle is to be used.

A person aged 17 or over may borrow a rifle from the occupier of private premises and use it only in his (or his employee's) presence on those premises provided that:
(1) A firearm certificate for the relevant rifle is held by the occupier of the premises or his employee, and:
(2) the person who borrows and uses the rifle complies with the conditions stated on the relevant certificate.

(c) *Licence to Kill Game*

Before a wild deer may be shot, a *Licence to Kill Game*, costing £6 per annum, must be obtained from a Post Office. A twelve month's licence runs from 1 August to 31 July.

(d) *Game Dealer's Licence and Venison Dealer's Licence*

Venison may only be sold to a licensed game dealer in England and Wales (*Deer Act* 1980) or to a licensed venison dealer in Scotland – *Deer (Amendment) (Scotland) Act* 1982. A licence to deal in game, valid for one year, is obtained from a Post Office after approval of the premises by the nearest District or Borough Council. A venison dealer's licence valid for three years can be obtained from any islands or district council.

(e) *Firearms and Ammunition*

(i) *England and Wales*
Deer Act 1991. *Rifles*. It is illegal to use any rifle against deer that has a calibre of less than .240 inches, or a muzzle energy of less than 2,305 joules (1,700 foot pounds).

Bullets must be soft-nosed or hollow-nosed. The following weapons are illegal: Airgun, air rifle, air pistol, arrow, spear or similar missile.

Shotguns. It is illegal to use any shotgun against deer *except* when authorised to do so in order to prevent serious damage to crops and growing timber etc. When authorisation is granted then the shotgun must be of not less than 12 bore gauge, and loaded only with either a single non-spherical projectile weighing not less than 350 grains (22.68 grams) or pellets of not less than size AAA.

(ii) *Scotland*
The Deer (Firearms etc.) (Scotland) Order 1985
Rifles. The main difference from the law in England and Wales is that no mention is made in the Order of a minimum calibre, but only to the performance of the bullet which must be soft-nosed. Bullet performances are defined which relate to those of the 50 grain (3.24 grams) .222 Remington load for Roe *only* and the 100 grain (6.48 grams) .243 Winchester for any species of deer.

The minima permitted under the Order are, therefore –

	Bullet Weight		Muzzle Velocity Feet per second (Metres per sec.)	Muzzle Energy Foot pounds (Joules)
	Grain	(grams)		
Any species of deer	100	(6.48)	2,450 (746.76)	1,750 (2,373)
Roe deer only	50	(3.24)	2,450 (746.76)	1,000 (1,356)

A few manufacturers, such as Norma, include this information on the cartridge carton but, unfortunately, not all, so reference will have to be made to their Ballistic tables.

Shotguns. Only in order to prevent serious damage to crops, pasture or trees etc. is it legal for the occupier of such land to use a shotgun, whose gauge must be of not less than 12 bore, against deer. It must be loaded with the following lawful ammunition:

All species of deer. Either a single rifled non-spherical projectile weighing not less than 380 grains (24.62 grams) or a cartridge containing pellets of not less than size SSG.

Roe deer only. A cartridge containing pellets of not less than size AAA.

(iii) *Northern Ireland*
Wildlife (Northern Ireland) Order 1985
Rifle. It is illegal to use any rifle against deer that has a calibre of less than .236 inches.

Shotguns. For the protection of crops and growing timber *only* may a shotgun be used on deer. It must be of not less than 12 bore gauge loaded with either a single non-spherical projectile weighing at least 350 grains (22.68 grams) or pellets of not less than size AAA.

(iv) *Eire*
Wildlife (Wild Mammals) (Open Seasons) Order 1979
Under the above mentioned Order, deer may only be shot with rifle, but for security reasons it is unlikely that any licence will be granted for a rifle of heavy calibre. A minimum bullet weight of 55 grains should be used. It is illegal to use a smooth bore shotgun for deer.

Appendix C

(a) *Medal categories for British Deer (Native and Exotic)*

	Bronze	Silver	Gold
Red deer (England)	165.00–179.99	180.00–194.99	195.00 and over
Red deer (Scotland)	160.00–169.99	170.00–179.99	180.00 and over
Roe deer	105.00–114.99	115.00–129.99	130.00 and over
Fallow deer	160.00–169.99	170.00–179.99	180.00 and over
Sika deer (Japanese)	225.00–239.99	240.00–254.99	255.00 and over
Sika deer (Manchurian)	300.00–349.99	350.00–399.99	400.00 and over
Muntjac	54.00–54.99	55.00–55.99	56.00 and over
Chinese Water-deer	150.00–159.99	160.00–179.99	180.00 and over

(d) Britain's Best Recorded Medal Trophies

Species	Country	Date	Length L cm.	Length R cm.	Inside span cm.	Beam L cm.	Beam R cm.	Wt.ø kg.a	No. of times LR	CIC score points	Shot by or present owner*
Red deer	Scotland	1981	100.5	108.4	94.0	13.2	13.6	4.75	7 + 7	185.09	W. Laurie
Red deer	England	1950	114.3	115.3	84.1	18.4	16.5	8.60	11 + 9	224.50	G. K. Whitehead*
Fallow deer	England	1985	68.8	72.3	–	–	–	3.95		204.34	Found dead
Fallow deer	England	1972	No details available							200.41	Dr. E. Ueckermann
Sika deer	Scotland	1982	53.8	57.8	37.8	8.3	8.0	–	4 + 4	252.80	G. K. Whitehead
Sika deer	England	1984	54.0	56.0	42.5	11.1	12.0	–	6 + 5	307.30	G. K. Whitehead
Sika deer	Ireland	c1984	57.3	58.5	34.4	9.9	11.1	–	4 + 5	289.40	Fr. Graf Waldburg
Muntjac	England	1986	12.8	13.0	–	4.3	4.3	–	2 + 2	70.10	Lt. Col. Lorimer
Muntjac	England	1980	13.5	13.9	10.2	3.5	3.8		2 + 2	68.00	Dr Newton
						Volume cc.		gm.			
Roe deer	Scotland	1976	27.8	28.4	10.3	340		733		203.35	P. Wilson
Roe deer	England	1971	25.0	26.0	8.9	365		750		210.25	M. J. Langmead
Chinese Water-deer	England	1984								220.00	G. Ashpole
		1984								220.00	D. Shipman

øWeight of antlers on frontal bone.   *Owner of trophy.

(c) What to Look for in a Trophy Head

(i) Red Deer Stag

A good Scottish head should have a length of about 91.4 cm. (36 in.), a beam of 12.7 cm. (5 in.), and an inside span of at least 76.2 cm. (30 in.). The classic type of head is a royal.

The longest recorded antler this century was on a 13-pointer from Braulen, Inverness-shire – 111.5 cm. (43⅞ in.) (1905). The widest inside span 101.6 cm. (40 in.) was on a stag from Bolfracks, Perthshire (1924). Sixteen or seventeen is about the maximum number of tines produced by a wild stag, but this number has been exceeded by ex-park stags released on the hill.

(ii) Fallow Buck

A medal trophy head should have good spellers, a palm width of 15 cm. (6 in.) or more, and an inside span of not less than 55 cm. (21½ in.).

(iii) *Roe Buck*
Any typically shaped 6-tine Roe head of·length about 22 cm. (8.7 in.) and weight of 500 gm. (16 oz.) or more will probably be approaching gold medal class.

(iv) *Sika deer Stag*
A typically shaped 8-tined head of length and inside span of about 55 cm. (21⅝ in.) and 40 cm. (15¾ in.) respectively will probably be in medal class.

(v) *Muntjac Buck*
A medal class head should have an antler length and inside span measurement of about 11 cm. (4⅜ in.) and 10 cm. (3¹⁵⁄₁₆ in.) respectively.

(vi) *Chinese·Water-deer Buck*
Medal class tusks should have about 58 to 60 mm. (2¼ to 2⅜ in.) exposed below the gum. The best tusks measured to date had a score of 220.00 CIC points (1984).

Note: For instructions how to measure under the CIC formula, reference should be made to the CIC book *The Game Trophies of the World* (1981), edited by G. Kenneth Whitehead, Werner Trense and A. J. Hettier de Boislambert.

Glossary

Note: All sports have their own peculiar terms and the following are the minimum required by the stalker of today. For a more complete Glossary, reference should be made to *Hunting and Stalking Deer in Britain Through the Ages* (see Bibliography).

Antler Deer have antlers – not horns

Bay Second point or tine of deer antlers

Beam Main stem of a deer's antler

Boss Base of antler – also coronet

Brow Lower or first point on a deer's antler above the coronet

Buck Correct name for male of Fallow, Roe, Muntjac and Chinese Water-deer

Burr Rough edge of coronet

Calf Correct name for young of Red and Sika deer

Cast Shedding of antlers

Clean When antler growth is complete and velvet discarded

Coronet Base of antler adjoining the *pedicle*

Crown or Cup Three uppermost points of a stag's antler in form of cup

Doe Correct name for female of Fallow, Roe, Muntjac and Chinese Water-deer

Fawn Correct name for young of Fallow, Muntjac and Chinese Water-deer

Gralloch The stomach and entrails of a deer

Grass Term sometimes used to denote killing a deer

Hind Correct name for female of Red and Sika deer

Hummel Male Red deer that never grows antlers

Imperial Name sometimes given to a 14-point stag, but no justification for it

Kid Correct name for young of Roe deer

'MacNab, John' Shooting a stag, and grouse, and catching a salmon all in one day

Mossed head Similar to perruque, the antler being hard, porous and light

Palm Palmated top of a Fallow buck's antlers

Pearling The roughness of the beam, particularly on Roe buck antlers

Pedicle The bone on the forehead from which the antler grows

Perruque Malformed antler growth resulting in mass of antler growth on Roe buck caused by injury to the testicles

Pluck Heart, liver and lungs

Point Each tine or projection sprouting from beam of antler

Royal Twelve-point stag's head with brow, bay and tray, and crown on top each side

Rut Mating season of deer

Shed Correct term for casting of antlers

Slot Track or footprint of deer

Spellers Points on palm of Fallow buck antlers

Stag Correct name for male of Red and Sika deer

Switch Head of four points (beam and brow only) or just two (beam only)

Target White rump of Roe in winter pelage

Tine Each point or branch emanating from beam of antlers

Tray The third point or tine on antlers of stag

Tush (or tusk) Canine teeth (when present) in upper jaw of deer

Tush (anal) Tuft of white hair developed on rump (target) of Roe doe in winter

Velvet Skin covering of antlers during growth

Wallow Place where a deer takes a mud bath

Yeld Hind that failed to calve the previous summer – not necessarily barren

Bibliography

The following are the most recent books dealing with the stalking and control of deer in Britain, and are recommended for further study.

A complete list of literature dealing not only with stalking but also with distribution and natural history of deer, will be found in my book *Hunting and Stalking Deer in Britain Through the Ages* (1980).

COLES, CHARLES (editor) *Shooting and Stalking – A Basic Guide* (London, Stanley Paul, 1983)

FOOKS, H. A. *Hints on Woodland Stalking* (British Deer Society, 1967)

KREBS, HERBERT *Young or Old*, Translated from German by Lt.-Col. Roy C. Harms (München, F. C. Mayer, Verlag, 1966)

LUXMOORE, EDMOND *Deer Stalking* (Newton Abbot, David & Charles, 1980)

PRIOR, RICHARD
Trees and Deer – How to Cope with Deer in Forest, Field and Garden (London, B. T. Batsford, 1983)
Modern Roe Stalking. Rhyl, Tideline Books, 1985

SMILLIE, IAN SCOTT *A Guide to the Stalking of Red Deer in Scotland* (London, Regency Press (London & New York), 1983)

SPRINGTHORPE, G. D. & MYHILL, N. G. (editors) *Forestry Commission Wildlife Rangers Handbook* (Forestry Commission, 1985)

WHITEHEAD, G. KENNETH
The Deer Stalking Grounds of Great Britain and Ireland (London, Hollis & Carter, 1960)

Deer Stalking in Scotland (London, Percival Marshall, 1964)
Hunting and Stalking Deer in Britain Through the Ages (London, B. T. Batsford, 1980)
The Whitehead Encyclopedia of Deer (Shrewsbury, Swan Hill Press, 1993)

Index